Fight my Monster

www.fightmymon

# MONSTROUS
## OFFICIAL
# GUIDE

**SIMON AND SCHUSTER**
First published in Great Britain in 2012
by Simon and Schuster UK Ltd
1st Floor, 222 Gray's Inn Road, London WC1X 8HB
A CBS Company

ISBN 978-1-4711-1570-7
Printed and bound in Italy
10 9 8 7 6 5 4 3 2 1
www.simonandschuster.co.uk
www.fightmymonster.com

# CONTENTS

# Greetings human!

You must be reading this because you know that **Fight My Monster** is an awesome online strategy card game. By using the different strengths and talents of your monsters, you can challenge other players to battle for nuggets, monster cards and of course, glory!

But **Fight My Monster** isn't just about having the biggest or scariest monster cards. It's about being clever and having brains too. Power is attained by practice and improving your skills. Losing can be just as important as winning. And Fate is always a probability.

Here's some other cool stuff you can do in the game:
• Create your own Monster playing cards
• Play with friends or make new ones
• Play minigames in the Arcade

## Now, the question is:

# ARE YOU READY TO FIGHT MY MONSTER?

# how to play

Getting in to Fight My Monster is easy.
Go online to: www.fightmymonster.com or www.monsterfun.com
Then, click on "**play now**" if you've never played before.
Do you already have an account? *Yes?*
Then why are you reading this page?!? Skip to page 14, human!

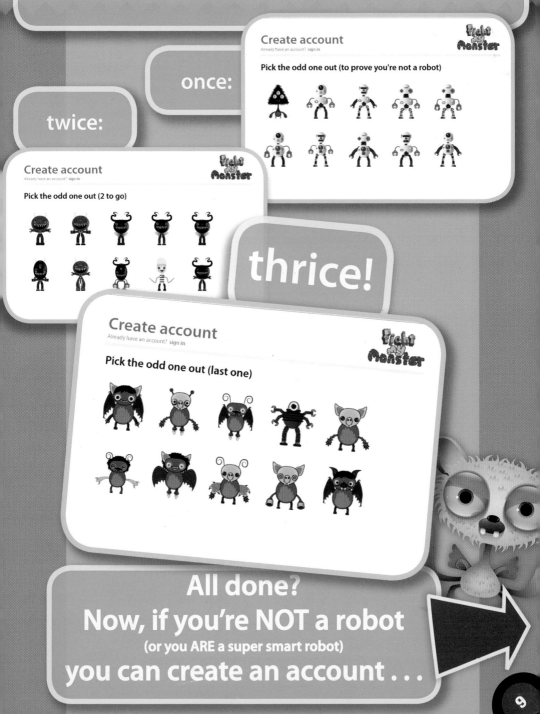

To play, you've got to prove you're not a robot. Robots are cool, but this game is for human players. You'll have to choose the odd one out . . .

once:

twice:

thrice!

**Create account**
Already have an account? sign in
Pick the odd one out (to prove you're not a robot)

**Create account**
Already have an account? sign in
Pick the odd one out (2 to go)

**Create account**
Already have an account? sign in
Pick the odd one out (last one)

All done?
Now, if you're NOT a robot
(or you ARE a super smart robot)
you can create an account . . .

# Ready to create your account?

## Great! First read these rules:

**1**

Be **nice** to others

**2**

No **cheating** or **scamming**

**3**

**Never** give out personal information!

**4**

**Never share your secret symbols with ANYONE!**

Easy peasy! Next step...

Choose a name you can remember - and make it **MONSTROUS**!

Now choose your secret symbols. Don't worry if you forget them, there's a handy reminder on the side. You can choose a theme for your page now or skip it.

# Create account

Already have an account? **sign in**

## Username and password

Choose a username that is not your real name and 4 secret symbols as a password...

Username  `discopig`

Password

click to change

Finish!

**forgotten?**

your secret symbols

We remind you of your secret password symbols on this computer until you activate your account

**Haaaaaaa!**   ✕

🖌 **Choose theme**
Choose a theme for your stuff. You can change later.

None

Monsters next. READY?

# Time to grow some monsters!

Your profile page is the first place you'll meet **Brawny the Informed**. Brawny will tell you to click on the **"Grow a monster"** card to grow a monster. You need nuggets to grow monsters. Luckily, if you check your mail, you'll see that **Grod, King of Fight My Monster**, has granted you 7,500 nuggets.

**All hail Grod!**

Hey, you need some monsters!

Click on standard growth and grow your first monster! It'll only cost you 100 nuggets. You'll also see that you've completed your first mission and Grod will pay you a visit. He'll also pay you 100 nuggets for completing your first mission, so your first monster is free!

Ready to FIGHT? Let's go!

# First FIGHT!

Once you've grown a monster, you'll probably get a challenge to fight! Click on your messages (in the top right corner of the screen) and check out the fight offer. Your message will look something like this:

1

**RedStorm** says to you
(4 minutes ago)

I challenge Mutant Bot LYSC2V to fight Sea Beast G1ZHN2.
Winner collects or eats the loser after 1 strategy round.
I offer you 5 nuggets to say yes :-)

See fight offer...    Say no!

Click on 'See fight offer' . . .

## Fight Offer

**Peche**                                    **RedStorm**

Mutant Bot LYSC2V            Sea Beast G1ZHN2

FIGHT ENDING
Winner Collects or Eats

STRATEGY ROUNDS
1

NUGGETS YOU WILL
BE PAID
5

Request more...

Vs

| | bonus | | | | | bonus | |
|---|---|---|---|---|---|---|---|
| 121 | 60 | 82 | 164 | | 74 | 37 | 24 | 48 |
| Attack | | total 524 | Defense | | Attack | | total 320 | Defense |
| Brains | | | Tricks | | Brains | | | Tricks |
| 121 | 60 | 59 | 118 | | 133 | 66 | 32 | 65 |

14

Since this is your first time, you can just keep clicking **'Yes...'** and **'Next...'** to whizz through the steps to start the fight. Just choose any strategy for now, we'll explain how all that works later.

Let **Brawny** guide you through your first **Fight My Monster** fight:

**121**
Attack

**164**
Defense

**total**
**524**

**Brains**
**121**

**Tricks**
**118**

Round 1! Choose a strategy! Unsure? Just try one!

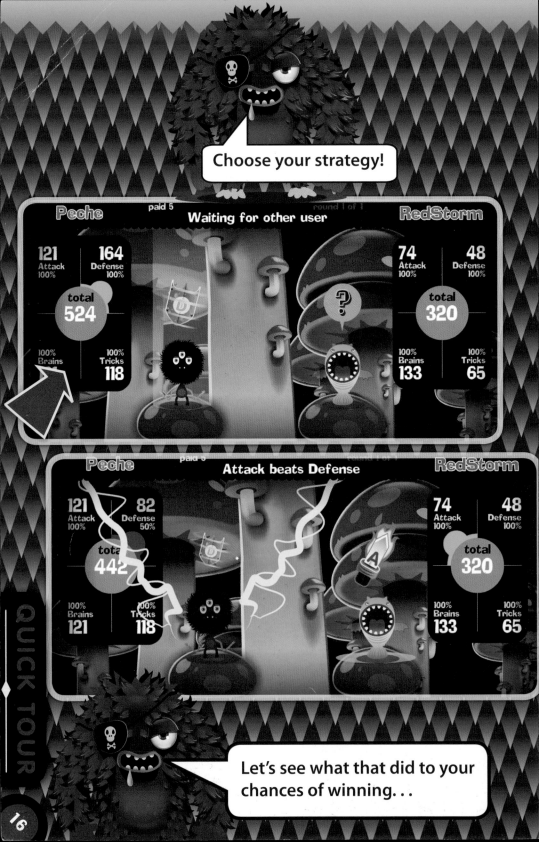

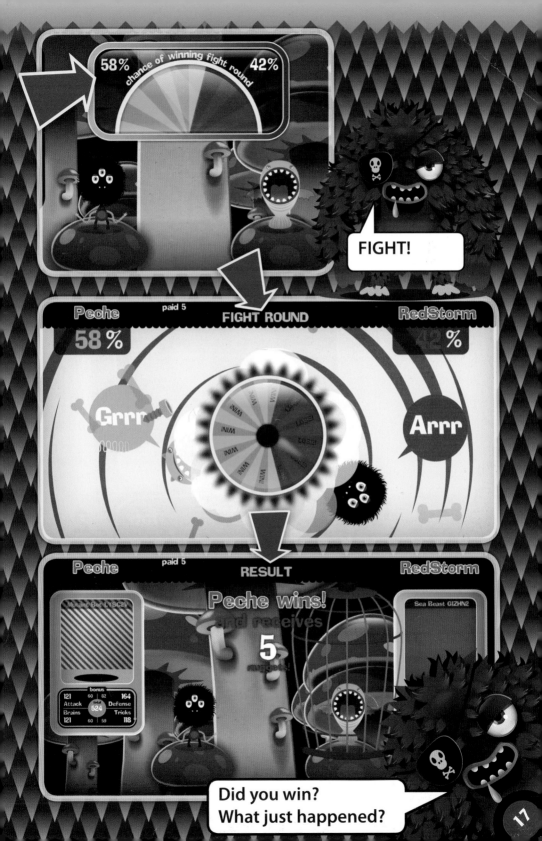

# Fight strategy

Now that you've played a little, you might have noticed that playing **Fight My Monster** is about strategy. Each monster has four different areas of strength:

Alien B10LXU

bonus

| 1 | 86 Attack | 43 | 78 | 156 Defense | 2 |

total 533

| 4 | Brains 221 | 110 | 35 | Tricks 70 | 3 |

The higher the points in an area, the stronger your monster is in that area. You want to play your monster's strength to win.

Don't worry if your monster's points are low – you can train them up to be stronger.

Stinger EYPJ14

Check out this stinger! Defense is his greatest strength. Remember
**k**=thousand
**m**=million
**b**=billion
**t**=trillion (yes!)

bonus
75 t | 37t | 69t | 138 t
Attack | total 397 t | Defense
Brains | Tricks
89 t | 44t

999999999999999

bonus
3 m | 1m | 1m | 2 m
Attack | total 11 m | Defense
Brains | Tricks
2 m | 1m | 1m | 2 m

The centre number is the total number of strength points your monster has. Click on it to see how many points you need to get to the next card level.

htujuj

bonus
37 k | 18k | 15k | 39 k
Attack | total 168 k | Defense
Brains | Tricks
41 k | 20k | 24k | 49 k

If your points flash red, the red numbers show what your monster's points are without the potion.

19

# Offers
## and consequences

Fight offers will appear in your messages. You can see them by clicking on the **messages** tab in the top right corner of the screen. Messages from Grod will appear here too. Click on '**See fight offer...**'

I challenge Fur Ball LL21SH to fight Mutant Bot T3E272.
Winner bites the loser after 2 strategy rounds.
I offer you 100 nuggets to say yes :-)

See fight offer...    Say no!

**Telemachus** says to you
(moments ago)

I challenge Sea Beast C3UBCS to fight Becky.
Winner bites the loser after 2 strategy rounds.
I offer you 50 nuggets to say yes :-)

**rottensatsu** says to you
(moments ago)

Before you fight your monster, you need to check what happens if your monster wins. But beware – whatever you choose will also happen to your monster if you lose. There are three choices:

## Bite, Collect or Eat.

STRATEGY

Peche

Telemachus

Fur Ball LL2ISH

Mutant Bot T3E272

**FIGHT ENDING**
Winner bites loser

**STRATEGY ROUNDS**
2

**NUGGETS YOU WILL BE PAID**
100

Request more...

Vs

| bonus | | | |
|---|---|---|---|
| 123 | 61 | 31 | 63 |
| Attack | total 512 | | Defense |
| Brains | | | Tricks |
| 157 | 78 | 84 | 169 |

| bonus | | | |
|---|---|---|---|
| 282 | 141 | 111 | 222 |
| Attack | total 735 | | Defense |
| Brains | | | Tricks |
| 117 | 58 | 57 | 114 |

CHANCE ■■■■■□□□□□

CHANCE ■■■■■□□□□

If you choose **Bite**, then a bite will be taken from the losing monster, and the monster will lose some of its strength. Each player keeps their monster.

If you choose **Collect** and you win, the losing monster will be added to your collection of monsters. But if you lose, your monster will be collected and you can't resurrect it.

If you choose **Eat** and you win, your monster eats the other monster and gains its strength and some of its bonus points! If your monster is eaten, you can resurrect it!

## Strategies next. READY?

# Strategy

Strategy rounds enable you to weaken the other monster before the main fight. The weaker the other monster is during the main fight compared to your monster, the better your chance of winning!

| 100 | 100 |
| Attack | Defense |
| 100% | 100% |

**total**
**400**

| 100% | 100% |
| Brains | Tricks |
| 100 | 100 |

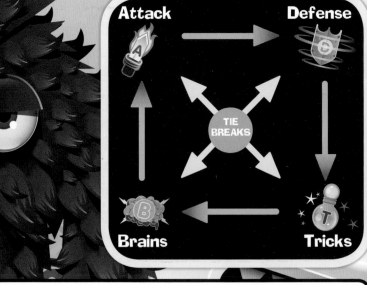

Attack → Defense

TIE BREAKS

Brains ← Tricks

Going clockwise around the card, each strategy ALWAYS beats the next strategy. In a tie break, the monster with the most points in that strategy wins the round.

Each strategy round, players choose **Attack**, **Defense**, **Tricks** or **Brains**. Grod recommends everyone thinks of these like the game 'Rock, Paper, Scissors' but more outrageously unspeakable.

**Attack** beats **Defense**
**Defense** beats **Brains**
**Tricks** beats **Brains**
**Brains** beats **Attack**
**Attack** and **Tricks** tie break
**Defense** and **Brains** tie break

Each round you win increases your chances of winning the overall fight. Watch the wheel to see how much your chance has changed:

14%     chance of winning     86%

**Max your Attack!**

# Strategy: Max Attack

When you choose **Attack** as your strategy, your monster digs deep and goes Super Rawr with an all out offensive attack. If you choose Attack and your opponent chooses Defense, no matter what the points, **Attack** always beats **Defense**.

**Attack** beats **Defense**
**Attack** tie breaks with **Tricks**
**Attack** draws with **Attack**
**Brains** beats **Attack**

Grod makes sure that monsters are equally matched in fights. If a really high level monster tries to fight a lower level monster, the fight offer will be blocked. All hail Grod.

Look at this fight. In this case, the best strategy for **Ice E5YDZ0** is **ATTACK!**

A

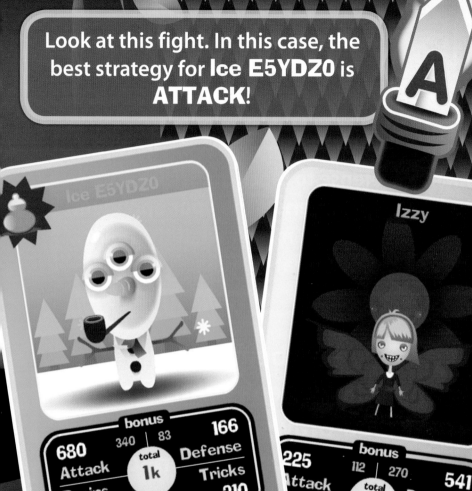

Ice E5YDZ0

bonus
340 | 83

**680**
Attack

total
**1k**

**166**
Defense
Tricks

Brains
**112**

56 | 105

**210**

Izzy

**225**
Attack

bonus
112 | 270

total
**1k**

**541**
Defense

rains
**245**

122 | 266

Tricks
**533**

If Ice E5YDZ0 chooses **Attack** and Izzy chooses **Tricks**, then it's a tie break and the monster with the most points in that strategy wins. In this match, Izzy's 533 **Tricks** points would win over Ice E5YDZ0's 680 **Attack** points.

# Strategy: Max Defense

When you choose **Defense** as your strategy, your monster calls upon its own shield of defense to block out tricksters. If you choose **Defense** and your opponent chooses **Tricks**, no matter what the points, **Defense** always beats **Tricks**.

**Defense** beats **Tricks**
**Defense** tie breaks with **Brains**
**Defense** draws with **Defense**
**Attack** beats **Defense**

You have 10 seconds to choose a strategy. If you don't pick one in time, one will automatically be chosen for you.

Behold another battle. In this case, the best strategy for Dominic is **Defense**!

**Dominic**

bonus
30 | 135

60 Attack

total **620**

**270** Defense

Brains

Tricks **82**

208
104 | 41

**Fur Ball QBIFO**

bonus
42 | 8

85 Attack

total **421**

**170** Defense

Brains 68

34 | 49

Tricks **98**

**Dominic** has a Tough Guy potion, which increases his **Brains** and **Defense** points x2. Monster cards with potions flash red to show the real points this monster would have without it. If **Dominic** didn't have the Tough Guy potion, this monster's best strategy would be **Brains**.

# Strategy: Max Tricks

Perhaps your monster is a shady Super Claw or a sly Slime Beast. If you choose **Tricks** as your strategy, and your opponent chooses **Brains**, no matter what the points, **Tricks** always beats **Brains**.

**Tricks** beats **Brains**
cks tie breaks with **Attack**
icks draws with **Tricks**
Defense beats **Tricks**

Strategies are reduced by 50% if a monster loses the round, so try to use this to reduce your opponent's highest strategy.

Time for another tussle. In this case, the best strategy for **Sea Beast RIHEUI** is **Tricks!**

**Sea Beast RIHEUI**

716 Attack
358 485 bonus 970 Defense
total 4k Tricks
Brains 809 404 1k 2k

382 Attack 191 258 bonus 517 Defense
total 2k
Brains 575 165 Tricks 330

Let's say that **Sea Beast RIHEUI** chooses its best strategy - **Tricks**, and **Devil E9P70M** chooses its best strategy - **Brains**. **Tricks** always beats **Brains**, so **Devil E9P70M**'s brains would go down 50%. If it happens again, **Devil E9P70M**'s **Brains** would go down to 0%. If it happens a third time, Devil E9P70M's next highest strategy will be reduced by 50%, so **Devil E9P70M**'s **Defense** would be reduced.

# Strategy: Max Brains

When you choose **Brains** as your strategy, your monster stuffs its oozing grey matter back into its head and actually thinks. If you choose **Brains** and your opponent chooses **Attack**, no matter what the points, **Brains** always beats **Attack**.

**Brains** beats **Attack**
**Brains** tie breaks with **Defense**
**Brains** draws with **Brains**
**Tricks** beats **Brains**

If your monster is stronger in every area, keep picking strategies that draw or tiebreak- you'll win more rounds this way.

Watch this brainy bash. In this case, the best strategy for **Mutant Bot S6FDV4** is **Brains!**

Mutant Bot S6FDV4

blast

**bonus**

| 3 (k) | 1k | 2k | 4 (k) |
|---|---|---|---|
| Attack | total | Defense |
| Brains | 20 k | Tricks |
| 6 (k) | 3k | 2k | 5 (k) |

**bonus**

| 5 (k) | 2k | 2k | 5 (k) |
|---|---|---|---|
| Attack | total | Defense |
| Brains | 21 k | Tricks |
| 4 (k) | 2k | 3k | 6 (k) |

If you're brainy like your monster, you know that part of the **Fight My Monster** game strategy is to guess what your opponent is going to do. **Blast's** best strategy is **Tricks** and they can see that **Mutant Bot S6FDV4**'s best strategy is **Brains.** Since **Tricks** beats **Brains, Blast** will most likely choose **Tricks.** But **Mutant Bot S6FDV4** might choose **Defense** instead to beat **Tricks.**

# FIGHTS IN-DEPTH

RoboPete

**bonus**

7 k
Attack

3k | 2k

4 k
Defense

total
21k

Brains
3 k

k | 2k

Tricks
5 k

Thinking about what strategy to choose is all well and good, but there's nothing like the experience of fighting to improve your game. You saw a taste of the game in the Quick Play Fast Fight, but here is how the fight actually plays out in all its glory!

Each fight has a minimum of 1 round or a maximum of 7 (if you're a member). You have to be ready to choose your strategy on your monster's card as the fight is happening.

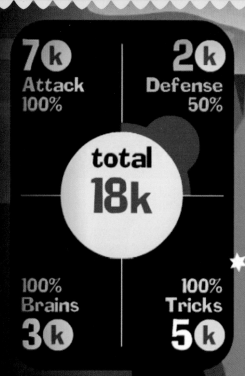

7k
**Attack**
100%

2k
**Defense**
50%

**total**
**18k**

100%
**Brains**
3k

100%
**Tricks**
5k

# round 1 of 4

## Attack beats Defense!

The loser of this round has the strategy
they played reduced by 50%.

7k Attack 100%

5k Defense 100%

total 22k

100% Brains 4k

100% Tricks 5k

45% chance of winning fight 55%

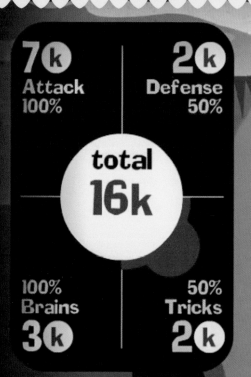

**7k**
Attack
100%

**2k**
Defense
50%

total
**16k**

100%
Brains
**3k**

50%
Tricks
**2k**

# round 2 of 4

## Defense beats Tricks!

The winner has their overall chance of winning the fight increased.

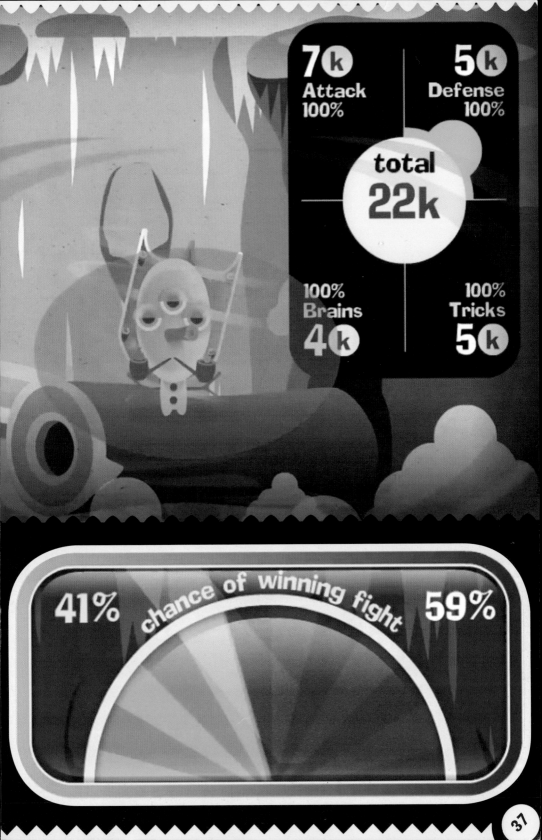

7 k
Attack
100%

5 k
Defense
100%

total
22k

100%
Brains
4 k

100%
Tricks
5 k

41% chance of winning fight 59%

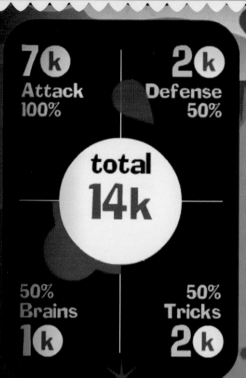

**7k**
Attack
100%

**2k**
Defense
50%

total
**14k**

50%
Brains
**1k**

50%
Tricks
**2k**

# round 3 of 4

## Tricks beats Brains!

The winner's overall chance of winning (in this case, the red section) increases again.

**3k**
Attack
50%

**2k**
Defense
50%

total
**10k**

50%
Brains
**1k**

50%
Tricks
**2k**

# round 4 of 4

## Brains beats attack!

What started as a 50%-50% match is now more in favour of **zombiepony** because he won the strategy rounds, but...

# ROUND!

zombiepony

68%

LOSE!
LOSE!
LOSE!
LOSE!
LOSE!

No matter what happens in the previous battle rounds, the wheel of chance determines who wins.

43

zombiepony wins!
and receives
200
nuggets!

WINNER!

RoboPete

bonus

| 5 (k) | 2k | 1k | 3 (k) |
|---|---|---|---|
| Attack | | | Defense |
| | total 15k | | |
| Brains | | | Tricks |
| 2 (k) | 1k | 2k | 4 (k) |

EHGombrich

bonus

| 9 (k) | 4k | 3k | 6 (k) |
|---|---|---|---|
| Attack | | | Defense |
| | total 28k | | |
| Brains | | | Tricks |
| 5 (k) | 2k | 3k | 7 (k) |

**RoboPete** has lost 6000 points as a result of his loss in this fight, but he does get to keep his bonus. Looks like he needs some more strategy practice!

As you can see, **EHGombrich's** points have increased by 6000! But since the chosen outcome was bite, they will both go on to fight another day…rematch?

Let's find some opponents!

# Ready to attack?

Now that you know how to play **Fight My Monster**, let's go find some worthy competitors. Look for the players tab at the top of your screen:

**Players**

The Players Map will show you everyone who is online. Players at the top half of the map are wealthy – meaning they have lots of nuggets. Players to the right half of the map are more active – meaning they've been playing lots. If you're looking for someone to challenge, someone on the upper right side of the map is good, with lots of nuggets to lose to your league of awesome monsters.

**Friends:** Find your friends easily by looking for the yellow helmets on the map.

**Members:** Got an Xtreme monster you're dying to put into battle? Look out for green helmets on the map. These are other **Fight My Monster** members.

You can click any player to go to their Profile Page.

**Country** – Check out who else is playing **Fight My Monster** around the world! Click on the flags to the right of the map, and players from that country will be highlighted. *Lutte mon monstre!*

Click a player                    Search

wealthy

idle                                                                active

The one in the black helmet is you!

I won a fight against LoopyDom

poor

| Anonymous | Activated | Friend | FMM Member |
|---|---|---|---|

# Lucky challenge!

Don't know who to fight? Check out the amazing **Lucky Challenge!** service, brought to you by fightmymonster.com! The Lucky Challenge automagically takes you through all of the steps involved in choosing who to fight. Then you decide the details of the fight offer. Here's how it works:

Go into your **messages** and click on **Lucky Challenge!** (near the top)

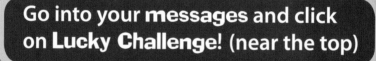

All        actions        talk        news

Lucky Challenge!  |  ☾ or |▢| to 11 friends

Now, sit back and watch while the website goes through these steps.

**1**

A player is chosen from the Player Map.

**2**

One of the player's monsters is picked for you to fight against.

**3**

Offer to FIGH
Challenge this monste

Ask to buy
Offer to pay nuggets fe

'Offer to fight' is selected from the three options

**4**

New Offer...

Select your monster

What d'ya think?

Your fight offer appears! Now you take over . . .

Next, make your offer...

# Offers

Way back on page **20** we saw what happens when you are sent a fight offer. Here's what to do when you're the one sending a challenge.

First, choose who to fight, either by **Lucky Challenge** or by clicking on a player on the Player Map. Now, select your monster! (Click on the white arrows to change cards).

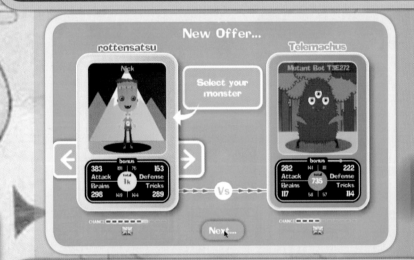

New Offer...

rottensatsu

Nick

Select your monster

Telemachus

Mutant Bot T3E272

bonus
383 | 191 | 76 | 153
Attack | | | Defense
Brains | 1k | | Tricks
298 | 149 | 114 | 289

Vs

bonus
282 | 141 | 81 | 222
Attack | | | Defense
Brains | 735 | | Tricks
117 | 58 | 57 | 114

Next....

Next, choose what happens to the other monster if you win. Your choices are:

## Bite, Collect or Eat.

These choices are explained on page **21**

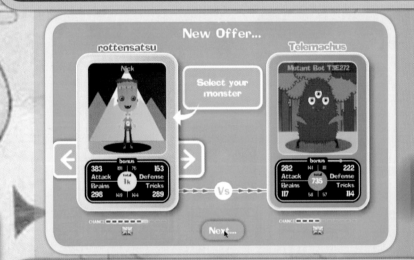

SETTING UP

50

Now, you need to decide how many of your precious nuggets to offer for the fight. Remember, you'll have to pay these nuggets even if you win!

Nuggets you will pay them to say yes

NUGGETS
36553

Next, choose how many rounds you want to battle. You can choose a minimum of 1 round and a maximum of 7.

Rounds of Strategy

3

Are you feelin' lucky?

## Review your fight offer:

rottensatsu

Nick

WINNER ACTION
Bite loser

STRATEGY ROUNDS
3

NUGGETS YOU WILL PAY THEM TO SAY YES
400

Telemachus

Mutant Bot T3E272

bonus
| 383 | 191 | 76 | 153 |
| Attack | | total | Defense |
| Brains | | 1k | Tricks |
| 298 | 149 | 144 | 289 |

Vs

bonus
| 282 | 141 | 111 | 222 |
| Attack | | total | Defense |
| Brains | | 735 | Tricks |
| 117 | 58 | 57 | 114 |

CHANCE ☐☐☐☐☐☐☐☐☐☐☐

CHANCE ☐☐☐☐☐☐☐☐☐☐

Send !!!

Happy? Click **Send!**

# Counter Offers

## Fight Offer

**Telemachus**                                    **rottensatsu**

Mutant Bot T3E272                                 Nick

FIGHT ENDING
**Winner bites loser**

STRATEGY ROUNDS
**3**

NUGGETS YOU WILL
BE PAID
**400**

Request more...

| | bonus | | |
|---|---|---|---|
| 282 | 141 | 111 | 222 |
| Attack | total 735 | | Defense |
| Brains | | | Tricks |
| 117 | 58 | 57 | 114 |

| | bonus | | |
|---|---|---|---|
| 383 | 191 | 76 | 153 |
| Attack | total 1k | | Defense |
| Brains | | | Tricks |
| 298 | 149 | 144 | 289 |

If you want to counter an offer, click on **Request more...** and name your price!

You can't change the number of rounds the challenger has set, but you can choose to **Eat** instead of **Collect** or vice versa.

Go on, ask for more...

SETTING UP

If someone counters your offer, you can view the amount of nuggets they want from you to fight. If it's too much, you can withdraw your fight offer by going back to the message and clicking **Say no!**

Say what they must pay you to fight

NUGGETS

500

I will fight Mutant Bot T3E272 against Nick.

Winner bite the loser after 3 strategy rounds.

But only if you pay me 500 nuggets...

See request...    Say no!

If you are happy to pay more, click **See Request** to go to the fight!

Nuggets Request

rottensatsu                                    Telemachus

Nick                                    Mutant Bot T3E272

WINNER ACTION
Bite loser

STRATEGY ROUNDS
3

NUGGETS YOU AGREE
TO PAY
500

| | bonus | | |
|---|---|---|---|
| 383 | 191 \| 76 | | 153 |
| Attack | total | | Defense |
| Brains | 1k | | Tricks |
| 298 | 149 \| 144 | | 289 |

| | bonus | | |
|---|---|---|---|
| 282 | 141 \| 111 | | 222 |
| Attack | total | | Defense |
| Brains | 735 | | Tricks |
| 117 | 58 \| 57 | | 114 |

Vs

CHANCE ⬛⬛⬛⬛⬛⬛⬛⬜⬜⬜        CHANCE ⬛⬛⬛⬛⬜⬜⬜⬜⬜⬜

FIGHT !!!

# Account types

Okay, so before you get excited about the battles you're going to have and the monsters you're going to grow, you may have noticed that there are some things you can only do if you've registered your account with an email address to activate it, or if you've convinced your parents to buy you a membership (because you've done all your homework and have cleaned your room, of course.) Here's a breakdown of what you can do with each type of account. We'll tell you more about each of these features in the next pages.

Check out the membership section of the website to find out how you can become a member...

| Account features | Anonymous: | Activated: | Member: |
|---|---|---|---|
| Fight | ✓ | ✓ | ✓ |
| Send fight offer | ✓ | ✓ | ✓ |
| Send buy offer | ✓ | ✓ | ✓ |
| Grow a standard monster | ✓ | ✓ | ✓ |
| Grow a super growth monster | ✗ | ✓ | ✓ |
| Grow an Xtreme Growth monster | ✗ | ✗ | ✓ |
| Sell monsters to Fast Eddie | ✓ | ✓ | ✓ |
| Buy monsters at the Market | ✓ | ✓ | ✓ |
| Design your own monster | ✗ | ✗ | ✓ |
| Buy potions from Potions Pete | ✓ | ✓ | ✓ |
| Resurrect dead monsters | ✓ | ✓ | ✓ |
| Play mini games in the arcade | ✗ | ✓ | ✓ |
| Choose a homepage theme | ✓ | ✓ | ✓ + more themes! |
| Create tribes | ✗ | ✓ anyone can join your tribe | ✓ your tribe is invite-only |
| Invite other people to your tribe | ✗ | ✓ | ✓ |
| Nudge other players | ✓ | ✓ | ✓ |
| Make friends with other players | ✗ | ✓ | ✓ |
| Send messages to other players | ✗ | ✓ if they are your friends and they're online | ✓ if they are your friends and they're online |
| Instant chat with other players | canned chats only :( | chat to friends in your own words! | chat to friends in your own words! |

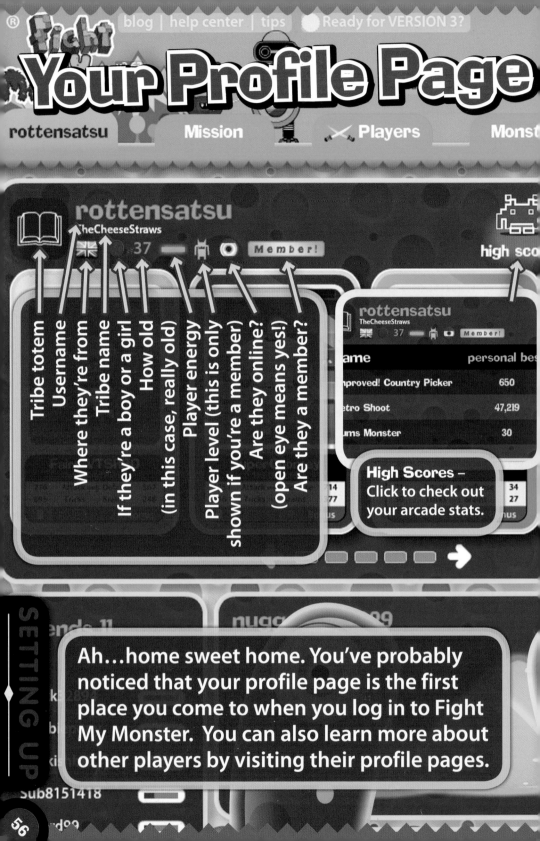

high scores    album    r-i-p

to move cards    drag to move cards
Show your album in normal mode

**Album** – Move your monster cards around in your album by clicking on the arrow. The first four will show on your profile page. Click on the arrow again to show your album in normal mode.

album    r-i-p

Theme
Settings

Themes    Account

Password    Change password
Blocked players    Managed blocked
Creature sounds    Creature sound OFF
Error log    Show error log
System Info    Show

rottensatsu
TheCheeseStraws
37    Member!

rottensatsu
(logout)

energy 100%
73 from 73 max

56,029
nuggets

RANK

Alien GI30GV    Fairy VTSRRO
died 26.07.12    died 20.06.12

friends 11

history

ONLINE

Telemachus

**Themes and Settings** – Make your profile page your own with these cool backgrounds. Some of these are for members only. You can also click on "Account" to change your password or block people if someone is bugging you. Don't forget – the Fight My Monster Crew are always roaming around looking out for people breaking the rules.

**RIP** – No monster is ever really dead. If your monster is eaten, you can resurrect it! But for a certain amount of nuggets, of course.

Energy left
Total nuggets
Your friends
Fight history
List of friends
Who are online

Don't worry about the Error log or System Info. This is Egg's stuff.

# The Circle of Goo

= nuggets

You need nuggets to buy monsters and to send fight challenges. So how do you get more nuggets?

**Missions**
**Membership**
**Arcade**

**Missions** – Grod will grant you nuggets if you complete your current mission. The higher level the mission, the higher the reward is. The best bit is that after you complete a mission, Grod will grace you with his presence. All hail Grod.

**= monsters**

Also, becoming a **member** helps. As a member, if your monsters and nuggets get too low, Fight My Monster Insurance gives you 25,000 new nuggets within hours. Members can never be wiped out for too long!

And of course, playing the **arcade** games will earn you nuggets as well. Check out the different games later in this book.

Winning a **battle** doesn't always mean you win the nuggets too. The human that sends the fight offer agrees to pay nuggets to the human they have challenged, whether they win or lose.

**= fights**

# Friends

You may be battling monsters, but those worthy opponents may be people you want to be friends with. You can practise battles, share fight strategies or send your favourite videos. **Fight My Monster** is a cool way to make new friends.

If you go to someone's profile page, on the right side are options for you to choose:

Nudge! ⇥

Instant chat ⓣ

Message ☰

Make friends ⪢

Invite to tribe ✉

Nudge - You send →

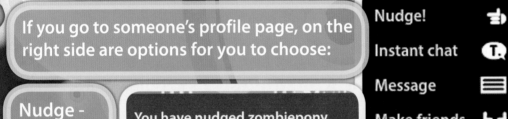

You have nudged zombiepony

OK

They get →

rottensatsu said to you
(9 minutes ago)

I nudge you !!!

close

Instant Chat - If a player is online, you can chat with them now! If you're friends with that player already, you can write what you like. The name at the top of the box is the person you are writing to. Just type in the bottom box, click on the emoticons if you want to add one, then click "send".

**rottensatsu** BLOCK

rottensatsu
Join my tribe!

Telemachus
Why should I?

rottensatsu
We can train together.

Cool.

**Your instant message will pop up on their screen like this**

---

**Telemachus** BLOCK

I like your monsters!

Challenge me if you dare!

Look at my monsters for sale

I've sent you a friend request

I've sent you a fight challenge

I've sent you a monster offer

How are you?

I'm a little blue

I'm feelin' good

I'll think about it...

No thanks

Thank you!

Bye! → CANC...

---

**If you're not friends with a player and you want to instant chat while you're both online, you can still send a ready-made message using this menu.**

---

**Message - If a player isn't online (or even if they are), you can send a message that will appear in their mail.**

message to Telemachus
You need more monsters!

→ SEND

---

**Make friends – If you want to be friends with a player on Fight My Monster, click on the "Make Friends" icon and this is what you'll see:**

Your offer of friendship has been sent to Telemachus

OK

**They get**

I want to be friends
YES become friends    No thanks

rottensatsu says to you
moments ago

---

**Invite to tribe - Tribes are groups of players that work together for glory points. You can invite other players to your tribe or even make your own!**

Invite to tribe ✉

Tribe invitation sent

OK

# TRAINING

# Create your own monster crew

You need a team of monsters to battle, because you never know when the wheel of chance is going to land on you or not. **Brawny the Informed** recommends having about 10 monster cards. If one has a bad battle, you've got more to play. Grow, build, trade or buy your monsters to make your ultimate crew. Then train them up to be supreme.

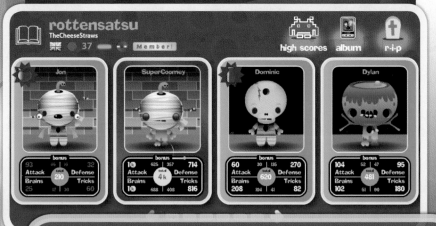

rottensatsu
TheCheeseStraws
37 · · · Member!
high scores  album  r·i·p

| Jon | SuperCoomey | Dominic | Dylan |
| --- | --- | --- | --- |

**rottensatsu** grew these ghastly Undead monsters. They all began as green level cards, but **SuperCoomey** is now a red level. She needs to battle other players with **Jon, Dominic** and **Dylan** to train those monsters up as well.

**mayfair**
blacktigerwarriors2

15  Member!

high scores   album   r-i-p

raygun

| bonus | | |
|---|---|---|
| 11 Attack | 5m 4m | 8 Defense |
| Brains | total 37m | Tricks |
| 9 | 4m 3m | 7 |

flashenBot ZXVCVL

| bonus | | |
|---|---|---|
| 11 Attack | 5m 3m | 7 Defense |
| Brains | total 32m | Tricks |
| 7 | 3m 2m | 5 |

AquaMILNE

| bonus | | |
|---|---|---|
| 11 Attack | 5m 3m | 7 Defense |
| Brains | total 34m | Tricks |
| 8 | 4m 3m | 6 |

Devil X7A65I

| bonus | | |
|---|---|---|
| 14 Attack | 7m 4m | 9 Defense |
| Brains | total 43m | Tricks |
| 10 | 5m 4m | 8 |

**Mayfair's** monsters all have strength points in the millions! Mayfair's been buying these Galaxy Burst level monsters or winning them in collect battles.

**bombsquad**
True_Gangsters_

14  Member!

high scores   album   r-i-p

Aqua LWHIAH

| bonus | | |
|---|---|---|
| 3 Attack | 1k 1k | 2 Defense |
| Brains | total 12k | Tricks |
| 3 | 1k 1k | 3 |

Spirit PZVP8N

| bonus | | |
|---|---|---|
| 85 Attack | 42m 34m | 69 Defense |
| Brains | total 261m | Tricks |
| 62 | 31m 22m | 45 |

KingYoshi

| bonus | | |
|---|---|---|
| 7 Attack | 3m 2m | 4 Defense |
| Brains | total 20m | Tricks |
| 5 | 2m 1m | 3 |

enter name

| bonus | | |
|---|---|---|
| 10 Attack | 5m 3m | 7 Defense |
| Brains | total 32m | Tricks |
| 8 | 4m 3m | 6 |

**Bombsquad** is mixing it up with monsters of different levels and strengths. **Spirit PZVP8N** is a Chemical Tsunami level, and can cost over 2 billion nuggets in the monster market.

# Grow Monsters!

You grew a standard monster when you first started playing. But you can also grow super monsters if your account is activated and Xtreme monsters if you are a member. From your Profile Page, go to the end of all your monster cards, and this card will be there.

## Grow a monster

**standard**
100 nuggets

**super**
1,000 nuggets

**Xtreme**
10,000 nuggets

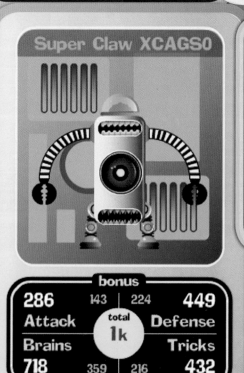

### Super Claw XCAGS0

| | bonus | | |
|---|---|---|---|
| **286** | 143 | 224 | **449** |
| Attack | total | | Defense |
| Brains | 1k | | Tricks |
| **718** | 359 | 216 | **432** |

Super growth monsters start out as yellow level monster cards. It might even come with bonus points already!

Xtreme growth monsters start out at blue level. A monster like this may cost you 10,000 nuggets, but they can be sold for over 20,000 nuggets in the Monster Market depending on its strength points.

**Mutant Bot WMD26N**

bonus

| | | |
|---|---|---|
| 1k | 990 | 3k | 6k |
| **Attack** | total **13k** | **Defense** |
| **Brains** | | **Tricks** |
| 3k | 1k | 869 | 1k |

If you want to sell, buy, build a monster or give it a potion, Monster Central is where it's at. Click on the "Monster Tab" at the top, which will take you there.

MONSTER CENTRAL

MONSTER TRADER    MONSTER MARKET    MONSTER BUILDER    POTION SHOP

You can also grow super or Xtreme monsters in the Monster Builder. Turn the page...

# Monster Trader

If you're short on nuggets or want to whittle your monster cards down to your fiercest fighters, visit the Monster Trader or Monster Market. Fast Eddie will offer you nuggets for your monster. The stronger your monster is, the more nuggets he'll offer.

MONSTER TRADER

# Monster Market

You can buy monsters at the Monster Market. The monsters for sale are shown by monster card level. Click on a monster you want to buy to find out more about their fight history.

## Monster Market

Available Green cards...

Refresh

To sell, go to your profile page and click on any of your monsters. Choose "Offer for Sale" and name your price.

Virus WYOMOM

**Offer for sale**
Choose a price for this monster.

**Profile**
Find out more about this monster.

Monsters for sale will have the red "for sale" sign on them in your profile. Other players' profile pages will also have their "for sale" signs on them. Or you can always offer to buy a player's monster.

# Monster Levels

Each monster card has a colour or pattern that indicates the level of your monster. You can level up a monster by winning a bite or eat fight. If you collect another monster in a battle, your monster level stays the same, but you add the monster card that lost to your collection.

1. Green
2. Yellow
3. Orange
4. Red
5. Purple
6. Blue
7. Grey
8. Black

9. Hyper Blue
10. Hyper White
11. Hyper Power
12. Hyper Power Xtreme
13. Iron Horse
14. Energy Wave
15. Neptune's Water

Don't forget – even if you have a Grod Energy Blue card, there's always the **Wheel of Chance** that determines the fate of the fight.

Don't be afraid to fight your monster against another monster of a higher level, but remember, Grod likes a fair fight, so monsters above **Kaleidoscope** level won't be able to fight monsters below **Blue** level!

16. Neptune's Water Xtreme

17. Plasmacore

18. Alien Power

19. Kaleidoscope

20. Galaxy Burst Black

21. Galaxy Burst Grey

22. Galaxy Burst White

23. Chemical Tsunami

24. Wormhole

25. Quark Power

26. Dark Matter

27. Grod Energy Yellow

28. Grod Energy Red

29. Grod Energy Blue

# Monster Builder
## Create Custom Monsters

The Monster Builder is awesome. You can build your own monsters, but only if you're a member.

MONSTER BUILDER

enter name

Click on monster parts to change them

by rottensatsu

Click on the green circle to change the type of monster.

enter name

Click on monster parts to change them

When you find one you like, click on the different body parts to change that feature.

When you're happy, give your new monster a name and then click on the check mark.

Stinkypoo

Click on monster parts to change them

Grow option

standard
100 nuggets

TRAINING

Select standard, super or Xtreme growth, just like you would from your profile page. Now your custom monster is ready for battle!

bonus
37 | 24
total
351
48
Defense

# Potions

If you want to give your monsters an extra boost, then visit Potions Pete in the Potions shop.

| Demon Attack | Tricks Maker | Tough Guy | Advantage Killer |
|---|---|---|---|
| **100 nuggets** | **100 nuggets** | **250 nuggets** | **500 nuggets** |
| Increases Attack x4 Lasts for 2 fights | Increases Tricks x4 Lasts for 2 fights | Increases Brains + Defense x2 Lasts for 2 fights | Cancels Opponent's Advantage Lasts for 3 fights |

| Mysterio | Incredible Hulk | Mysterio Rage | Giant Slayer |
|---|---|---|---|
| **1,000 nuggets** | **2,000 nuggets** | **3,000 nuggets** | **5,000 nuggets** |
| Increases Attack + Tricks x 2 Your opponent can't see the odds, so your advantage is a mystery (hence the name!) | Increases All powers x 4 Lasts for 5 fights **Members Only!** | Increases Attack and Tricks x 5 Your opponent can't see the odds Lasts for 2 fights **Members Only!** | Your opponent's powers are decreased x10 Lasts for 3 fights **Members only!** |

Choose your potion first, then choose the monsters that gets it.

# Training Tips

## Build a Team of Monsters

You never know how your battle is going to turn out, so it's best to have about 10 different monsters. This way, you can fight your strongest monsters against tough opponents, or try fighting your lower level monsters in more friendly matches.

## Train with Friends

Grod recommends building up fights for your monster. The more you win and build your bonuses, the stronger your monster card will become. Many players form tribes and work on training their monsters in friendly matches that help them and their monsters gain monster experience.

## Bite Only Fights

When you're first learning the different ways to play fight my monster, you can offer or counter fight offers with bite as the end result. This way, you don't lose any of your monsters and you can still increase the level of your monster card with a bite fight.

## Practise

Even if you know that Attack beats Defense and Tricks beats Brains, there's nothing like practising to help you become a better player. Practise using different strategies to increase your chances of winning.

Top Tip: listen to ME!

## Develop an Instinct

To win battles, you also need to think about what strategy your opponent is going to choose to help decide what you should pick. Just like playing 'Rock, Paper, Scissors', sometimes you get a gut feeling about what someone else is going to do. The only way to improve this skill is by playing against other humans.

## Level Up

The more you play a card, the more bonuses and wins you get, which will make your card level higher. Through determination and dedication, you too can have a Grod Energy level card.

# Bonus Points

Your monster card has bonus points that are added to every time you win a fight. The white border around your monster's strength points gets filled in every time you win. The closer the border is to being filled, the closer your monster card is to receiving the bonus points in your bonus pot.

Fur Ball GEJZDD

bonus

619k | 447k | **895** k

1 m
Attack

total
**4 m**

Defense

Brains
1 m

515k | 425k | **851** k

Tricks

# Bonus Pot

## When this monster wins:

## 2

more fights then its bonus pot will be added to its strength making it much stronger.

Winning hard fights makes the bonus pot grow bigger.

**bonus**

## 846k

Hold your cursor anywhere over the bonus border and you'll see exactly how many fights you have to win and how many bonus points are in your monster's bonus pot. Your monster has to win 10 fights, and then on the next fight, the bonus pot is added to your monster's attributes. This can help your monster jump several monster card levels in one fight!

MONSTERS

Beasts are a powerful fighting species, known for their strength, intensity and wild behaviour. A fierce category of monster that often exhibits powerful attack levels, most Beasts prefer to roam alone. Only the Fur Ball is currently known to play well in packs. Most sub-species evolve with an abundance of thick body hair, but this isn't always the case (see Sea Beasts, Orcs and their kin). In battle, Beasts rely on their size and strength to dominate opponents. Nearly all variants are naturally bulky. This species seeks out extreme habitats. Beasts can be found dwelling in caves, on mountaintops and in the very deepest parts of the ocean.

**1**

**Dank green skin**

**2**

**Arms can mutate into many extreme forms**

**3**

**Stumpy toes help bear giant frame**

MONSTERS

**Orc HR3A2I**

bonus

185 🄺 | 92k | 66k | 133 🄺
Attack | total | Defense
Brains | 593 k | Tricks
144 🄺 | 72k | 64k | 129 🄺

Orcs are naturally tall in stature – a physical trait that causes them endless inconvenience. They find it extremely difficult to find clothes that fit properly, hence their tendency to roam in sackcloth tunics and uncomfortable trousers.

This sub-species generally lurk in caves, deep below ground level. As a consequence they are plagued with terrible health – most Orcs have bunged-up noses, waxy ears and aching bellies. When they climb up to the surface to scavenge or do battle, they don't fare much better. The dank Orc complexion is highly sensitive to sunlight, burning quickly if the Beast steps out of the shadows.

Orcs are not difficult to track. Although they spend the majority of their time hidden underground, these big, lumbering ogres can often be sighted hunting for food. Orcs have an almost insatiable appetite, requiring numerous meals every day. They can't afford to be choosy about their diet, devouring anything and everything they come across. This is understood to contribute to the Orc's offensive natural body odour – an overpowering stench that is likened to horse dung.

**Orc RGW420**

bonus

7 🄺 | 3k | 3k | 6 🄺
Attack | total | Defense
Brains | 26 k | Tricks
6 🄺 | 3k | 2k | 5 🄺

# BEASTS: FURBALLS

**1**

**Acute canine hearing**

**Mutates with one, two or three eyes**

**2**

**3**

**Sharp fangs for tearing food**

Ygraine

| bonus | | |
|---|---|---|
| 852 | 426  239 | 479 |
| **Attack** | total 2k | **Defense** |
| **Brains** | | **Tricks** |
| 979 | 489  217 | 435 |

Don't be fooled by their cute puppy eyes and fluffed-up ears, Furballs are fighting machines! These Beasts are stacked with muscles, bulking up a distinctive top-heavy body shape. Some Furballs even have the ability to fly.

Furballs are sociable creatures that play well in packs. They are born into large litters that stay together until the young are big enough to hunt and feed by themselves. Young Furballs are exceptionally noisy and inquisitive. Occasionally a sub-species of Furball develops that is smaller and weaker than usual. Although these runt-like strains are less powerful in battle, they make up for any physical shortcomings by displaying an increased intellect.

Just like the name suggests, Furballs are incredibly furry! They groom their coats regularly, taking enormous care to keep their pelt clean and dry at all times. At the first sign of rain, a Furball will scurry for shelter. The Beast's thick hair can take hours if not days to dry out properly, so any water is best avoided. A Furball with a soaked coat will spend all night howling.

adorablefuzzy

80
Attack
40
bonus
51
102
Defense
Brains
199
total
556
99
87
Tricks
175

**1**

Some mutations grow horns

**2**

Impressive wing span

**3**

Razor-sharp claws

MONSTERS

**zog**

| bonus | | | |
|---|---|---|---|
| 10 m | 5m | 3m | 6 m |
| Attack | | total | Defense |
| Brains | | 29 m | Tricks |
| 7 m | 3m | 2m | 5 m |

Dinosaur Age Beasts make terrifying fight opponents – their slashing claws, mighty size and flashing teeth have been known to send countless monsters running for the hills! This reptilian species is cold-blooded, with scaly skin and strutting, bird-like features.

Many Dinosaur Ages can fly with expert precision. Their large, fleshy wings unfold to reveal enormous spans. Not all of these Beasts are airborne, however. Many sub-species spend their days roaming on foot in search of prey. No matter how they mutate, all have a nest that they go back to every night. A Dinosaur Age likes to sleep in comfort – great care and effort is lavished into making sure that its nest is dry, clean and snug.

Despite their intimidating appearance, Dinosaur Ages display some surprising phobias. The Beasts are terrified of meteors, fleeing to their nests whenever the sky clouds over. They will shriek in panic at the mere sight of a cockroach. These complicated Beasts are also neurotic about the future of the species – any reference to the Ice Age will simply not be tolerated.

**Dino SIYG6M**

| | bonus | | |
|---|---|---|---|
| 42 | 21 | 47 | 94 |
| Attack | | total | Defense |
| Brains | | 350 | Tricks |
| 102 | 51 | 56 | 112 |

# BEASTS: SEABEASTS

**1**

**Eyes are effective at great depths**

**Over-sized mouth for taking in oxygen**

**2**

**3**

**Fins take many shapes**

Beware when you step into the water – not many emerge unscathed after an encounter with a Seabeast! Few realize that these aquatic giants are actually mammals, expertly mutated to reign supreme beneath the waves.

All Seabeasts need to come up the surface to take on oxygen from time to time, but they have become highly efficient at this. The species can take fill their lungs with enough air to survive underwater for huge periods of time. This means they are able to explore deep waters without fear of drowning.

Seabeasts are renowned for growing to massive sizes. This is because they often find themselves exploring lonely expanses of water where there are no natural predators to threaten their growth. If left to swim in peace, the species' lungs can grow to such a size the creature will only need to come up to the surface after dark.

For those that want to observe a Seabeast in its natural habitat, there are a number of regions where sightings are possible. The species is very partial to Lake Placid and the waters surrounding Scotland.

Sea Beast NOS4YO

bonus
17k    17k
34 Attack    total 146 k    34 Defense
Brains 35    Tricks 41
17k    20k

Sea Beast EDOJ02

bonus
860    1k
1 Attack    2 Defense
total 8 k
Brains 2    Tricks 2
1k    1k

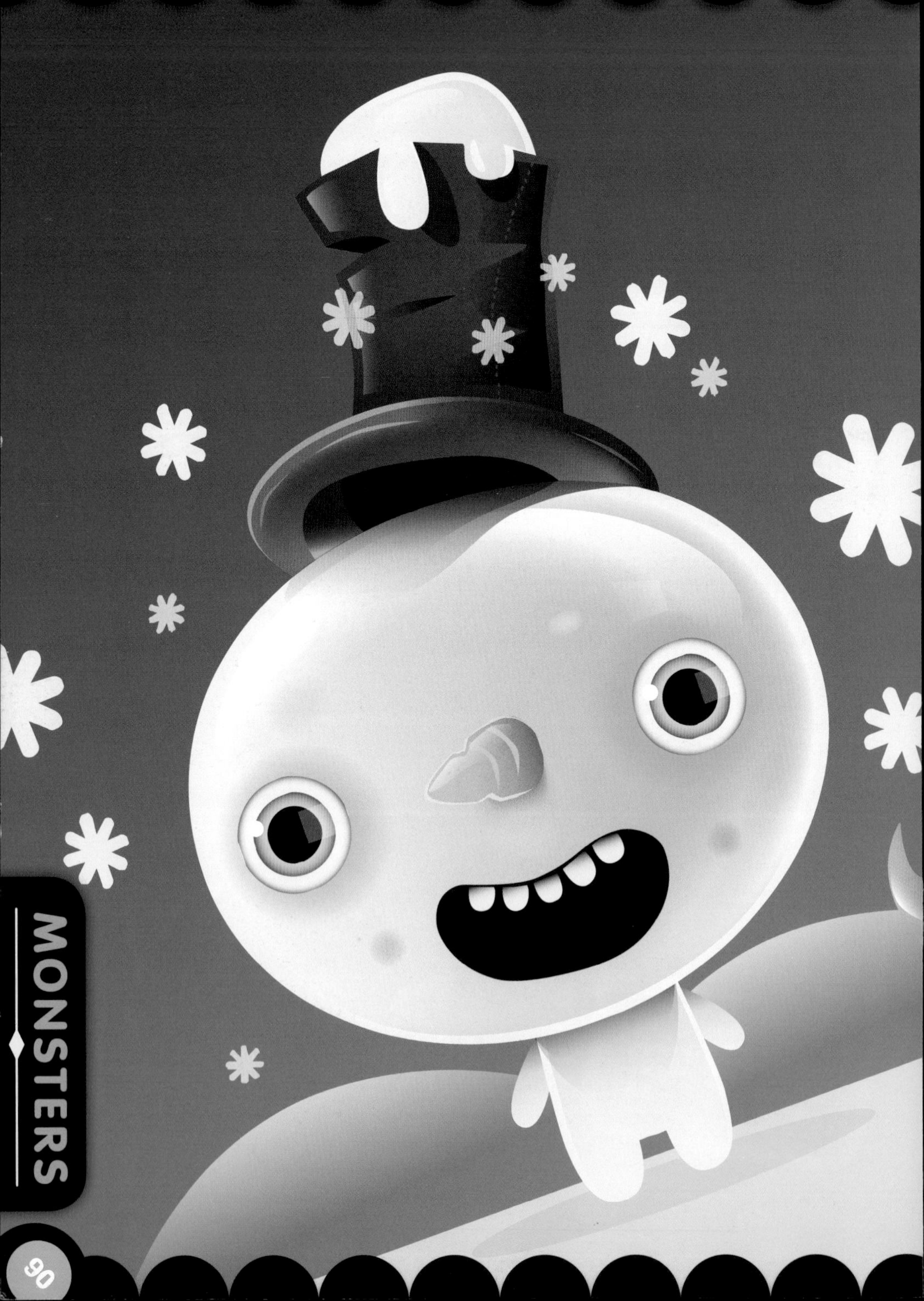

Perhaps our closest relations, Mutants are humanoids that have evolved and devolved into a staggering range of forms. The sheer breadth of this mutation is mind-boggling – from bitterly cold Ice Creatures to ever-multiplying Viruses. Every species is constructed from human parts or the mutation of an animal or human, proving just how ingenious nature can be! The study of Mutants can lead to fascinating results. Robot Mutants in particular can diversify into some crazy mutations. As would be expected, Mutants prefer to live in communities, the larger the better. Hundreds or even thousands of the creatures have been known to grow, mutate and breed within a single colony.

**1** Multi-coloured eyes

**2** Wings often purely decorative

**3** Unbalanced body parts

Mutant Pets are like human pets, but on a charged-up, super-sized scale! This extreme species are known to be sociable, friendly and even loyal at times. They are however, notoriously unpredictable. All mutations have a twisted blend of DNA running through their veins!

Mutant Pet B... MB8

bonus

1k    503    553    1k
Attack        total    Defense
Brains    4k    Tricks
1k    566    453    907

Mutant Pets are not your average household companions, but they can be fun to have around. Their sheer bulk make them tricky to contain if they get over-excited – the critters can wreak untold damage simply by not knowing their own strength! If kept inside, a steel cage is recommended to keep the Mutant out of trouble. With patience and time, it is possible to encourage some sub-species to control their incredible powers. They are difficult to house-train, but it can certainly be done.

The huge range of colours, shapes and forms can make Mutant Pets tricky to identify. Look out for googly eyes, goofy grins and rows of wonky teeth. Some sub-species will grow wings and feathers, but generally they are not able to fly.

Mutant Pet XGSN93

| | bonus | | |
|---|---|---|---|
| 142 m | 7lm | 88m | 177 m |
| Attack | total | | Defense |
| Brains | 556 m | | Tricks |
| 142 m | 7lm | 47m | 94 m |

**Pointy carrot-like nose**

**1**

**Crystal-white head**

**2**

**3**

**Icy-fresh breath**

Brrr! Ice Creatures lurk in the chilliest regions, in a constant quest to stay out of the sun. The species thrives in bitter climates, building up a diamond-like durability to frost, hail and snow blizzards. In most Ice Creature circles, 'thaw' is considered to be a highly offensive curse that is never repeated out loud.

This Mutant often evolves into humanoid forms. There is a good scientific reason for this – thinner Ice Creatures can be mistaken for icicles and easily snapped in two by predators. On cold days, the species will even roll in the snow to add girth and bulk to its frame. Many have twiggy arms and a pointy, carrot-like snout. Sometimes the tip of a nose poking out of a snowdrift is the only way of spotting an Ice Creature in its natural habitat.

Even though it can live a lonesome existence, an Ice Creature likes to looks after its appearance. The Mutant will scavenge hats to wear and even pilfer a scarf or set of buttons. It is also very proud of its pleasant, crisp breath.

Ice IOKWFJ

bonus
87  43 | 98  196
Attack  total 392  Defense
Brains  Tricks
52  26 | 28  57

Ice QC0I6E

bonus
87  43 | 55  111
Attack  total 434  Defense
Brains  Tricks
96  48 | 70  140

# MUTANTS: ROBOT MUTANTS

**1** Reinforced steel body

**2** Multiple rows of teeth

**3** Eyes wired direct to brain

MONSTERS

Mutant Robots are a curious example of nature and machines working as one. Chrome, cable and automated circuit boards combine with fur and flesh to create a sub-species that is astonishing in its variety. Animal faces peer out of metal visors and droids can be observed transporting themselves on nimble, humanoid legs. It is no surprise that these Mutants are distant relatives of the Robot race.

Experienced FMM strategists are often attracted to Mutant Robots. The species can exhibit the best of both robot and humanoid abilities. Their cast iron frame make them resilient to attack, while their natural instinct regularly comes up trumps in the field of battle. Most adversaries will back away when faced with a calculating Mutant Robot in a bad mood.

Mutant Bot QHZEWH

bonus

| | | |
|---|---|---|
| 2⟨k⟩ | 1k \| 1k | 2⟨k⟩ |
| Attack | total 10k | Defense |
| Brains | | Tricks |
| 3⟨k⟩ | 1k \| 1k | 2⟨k⟩ |

It is not surprising therefore that Mutant Robots are extremely elitist in their behaviour. They believe that they are an improvement on Robots, seeing themselves as the ultimate mutation upgrade. The species has got a reputation for being rude and standoffish, with very little time for anybody other than their own kind.

Mutant Bot S6FDV4

bonus

| | | |
|---|---|---|
| 3⟨k⟩ | 1k \| 2k | 4⟨k⟩ |
| Attack | total 20k | Defense |
| Brains | | Tricks |
| 6⟨k⟩ | 3k \| 2k | 5⟨k⟩ |

# MUTANTS: VIRUSES

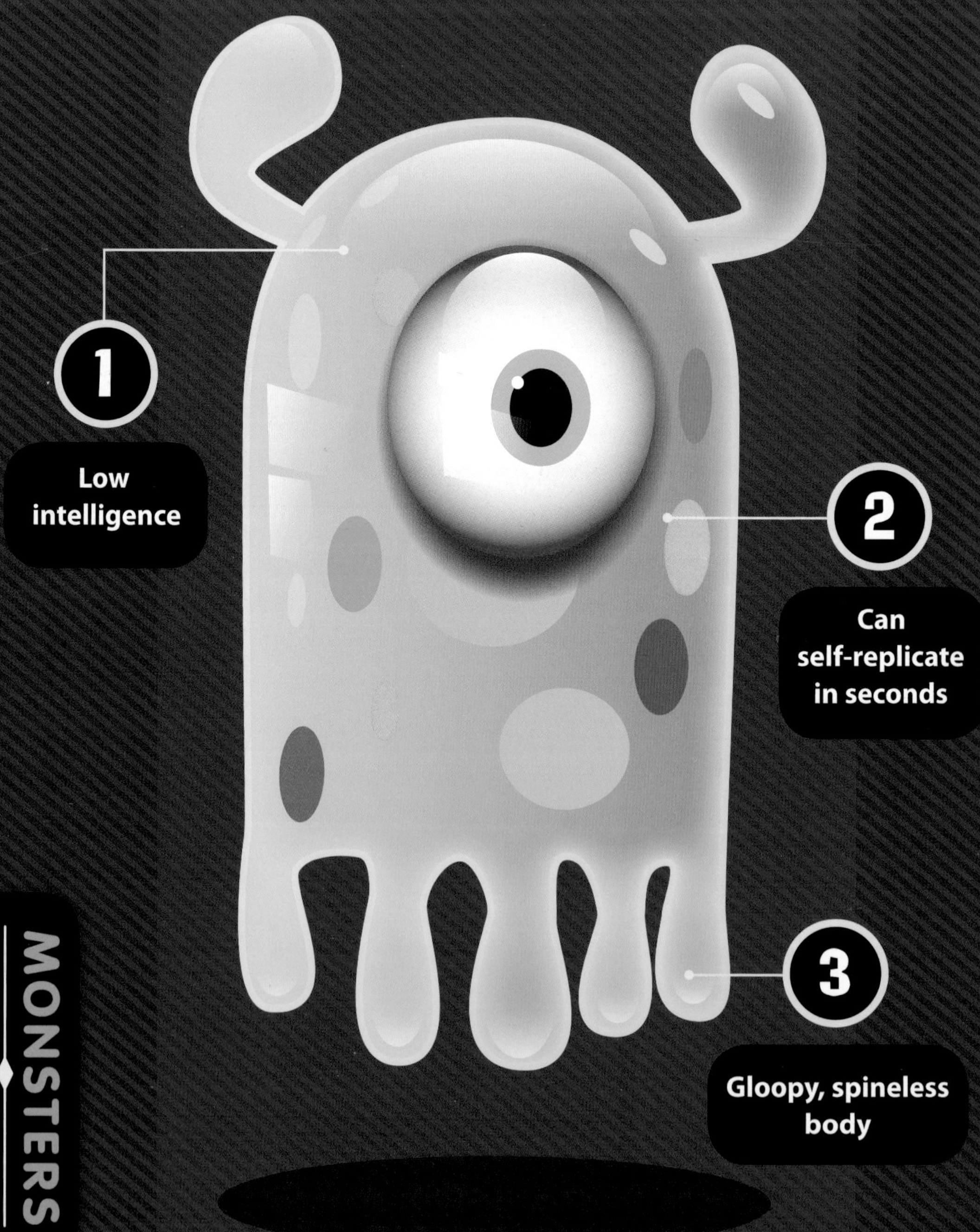

**1** Low intelligence

**2** Can self-replicate in seconds

**3** Gloopy, spineless body

**Virus PNILFQ**

| | bonus | |
|---|---|---|
| 5 (k) | 2k \| 613 | 1 (k) |
| Attack | total 13 k | Defense |
| Brains | | Tricks |
| 4 (k) | 2k \| 834 | 1 (k) |

No matter which way you look at it, Viruses are unpleasant little creatures. These Mutants contribute nothing to the FMM world apart from the ability to clog the place up by multiplying in their millions. The gooey sub-species has no ambition other than to hook up with other Viruses and create even more distorted copies of themselves. The critters breed and mutate at an alarming rate.

Just like most germs, Viruses thrive in warm, tepid locations. The creatures will flock together like cells on a petri dish, clustering their gooey bodies as close as they can. This natural instinct is too tough to resist – Viruses are not known for being individuals.

Although it can take on all manner of shapes, a Virus generally develops a large, gooey frame. The Mutant does not have a backbone, so its body can wobble and bend if it gets squashed into tight corners. Most other Monsters go all out to avoid getting close to Viruses for fear of getting one stuck to them. Luckily Viruses are too thick-skinned to give a hoot.

**Virus C9HDAV**

| | bonus | |
|---|---|---|
| 220 | 110 \| 86 | 172 |
| Attack | total 588 | Defense |
| Brains | | Tricks |
| 81 | 40 \| 57 | 115 |

'Earth calling Alien. Earth calling Alien. Take me to your leader!' Aliens are long-distance travellers with an unquenchable thirst for discovering strange new planets. It is still not clear whether this other-worldly species pick their journeys deliberately or simply get lost on a regular basis. The curious should beware: most advancing Aliens have only one thing on their minds – to isolate who's in charge and take over the place! This obsession with ruling anything and everything can land the species in all sorts of unnecessary trouble. Aliens can show up in the unlikeliest places! With a whole galaxy out there to explore, they're not going to stop roaming any time soon.

# ALIENS: SLIME BEAST

**1**

**Horns are soft and feeble**

**2**

**Mouth can mutate into many forms**

**3**

**Sticky skin is tricky to keep clean**

Slime H8KIKV

bonus

811k | 405k | 466k | 932k
Attack | total | Defense
Brains | 3m | Tricks
1m | 511k | 325k | 651k

If you spot a blobby, brightly-coloured critter floating through the sky, the chances are that it's a Slime Beast! This gelatinous form of Alien gloops around space, dropping in on random planets as the mood takes it. Although it will attempt to conquer any new environment that it comes across, the Slime Beast is rarely successful – most other species in the Universe don't take very kindly to the demands of such a sticky, spineless creature.

Slime Beasts match their beastly attitude with an equally beastly appearance. They have no desire to make friends with the new species that cross their path. In fact, they actively rub them up the wrong way.

Although these Aliens can mutate into all manner of shape, size and colour, their jelly-like bodies make them a cinch to spot. Slime Beasts are so wobbly and gummy, you can see right through them in certain lights. They are said to be a distant relative of 'The Blob'. Their icky sticky skin picks up dirt very easily, causing many Slime Beasts to tour the galaxy with all sorts of flotsam and jetsam stuck to their backs and behinds.

Virus C9HDAV

bonus

220 | 110 | 86 | 172
Attack | total | Defense
Brains | 588 | Tricks
81 | 40 | 57 | 115

**1**

**Eyes can stretch on stalks when required**

**2**

**See-through body**

**3**

**Flexible appendages can shrink and stretch**

Blend an unsuspecting Alien with a dollop of foreign materials and what do you get? Plasticos! This opaque species has the ability to stretch, bend and shrink just like melted plastic. They mutate into a rainbow of possible colourways, but all are virtually transparent. Peering into a Plastico's eyes is fascinating – you can see right through them and out the other side.

Plasticos are very useful creatures, changing their form to suit the needs of those around them. If they become bored, they have even been known to take on work as temporary food containers. Their pliable nature makes them adaptable to most environments, although they don't fare well in direct sunshine. Their skin is generally smooth and slippery, but too much heat will cause it to bubble up.

In battle, Plasticos always play to their strengths. Their mutated bodies can absorb intense blows without sustaining major damage. They can also smother opponents by stretching themselves until they're completely flat. If a situation becomes desperate, Plasticos have the flexibility to hide in tight spaces.

Plastico AJGUDX

bonus

| | 19b | 38b | |
|---|---|---|---|
| **39** b | | | **76** b |
| Attack | total | | Defense |
| Brains | **212** b | | Tricks |
| **48** b | 24b | 24b | **48** b |

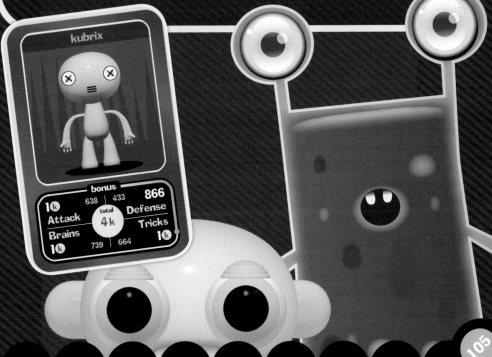

kubrix

bonus

| | 638 | 433 | |
|---|---|---|---|
| **1** k | | | **866** |
| Attack | total | | Defense |
| Brains | **4** k | | Tricks |
| **1** k | 739 | 664 | **1** k |

Would you have the courage to seek out a Fantastical on a dark, lonely night? Vampires, Devils and the Undead are the stuff of FMM folklore, strange mutations that are said to be distant relatives of the 'Original'. It is true to say that Fantasticals have one foot in this world and the other in some darker, gloomier sphere. Most are loners – nocturnal beasties that choose to lurk in the shadows when most regular Monsters are tucked up asleep. Devils and Spirits however take ghastly pleasure in connecting with their fellow species, even if that means leaving a trail of chaos in their wake.

**1**

Horns are
very common

**2**

Knife-like
teeth

**3**

Fire-resistant
body

MONSTERS

**Devil D0VW4C**

bonus

| 1🍷 | 562 | 532 | 1🍷 |
|---|---|---|---|
| **Attack** | **total 4k** | | **Defense** |
| **Brains** | | | **Tricks** |
| 1🍷 | 560 | 643 | 1🍷 |

They may smirk, wave and cackle with glee, but Devils are to be handled with great care. The wee little stinkers are bent on causing mayhem anywhere and everywhere! This species thrives on discord and anarchy, often hooking up with friends to spread that disruption far and wide. If you do spy a Devil up close, don't attempt to confront it. It is very likely to invade your home, before summoning the rest of its clan.

Devils often have red bodies, but they can mutate into any colour. Although they are active and nimble on their feet, a weak gene in the species can cause blood pressure issues. When faced with confrontation, these Fantasticals are ruthless biters. They use their keen eyes to spot their quarry, then go in with both jaws open, their razor-sharp teeth glinting in the light.

Unlike many Fantasticals, Devils are social critters that thrive in big, noisy communities. Large groups will choose to make their home inside live volcanoes, skipping expertly in and out of the splurting lava.

**Devil R9R0DD**

bonus

| 6🍷 | 3k | 3k | 6🍷 |
|---|---|---|---|
| **Attack** | **total 32k** | | **Defense** |
| **Brains** | | | **Tricks** |
| 9🍷 | 4k | 4k | 9🍷 |

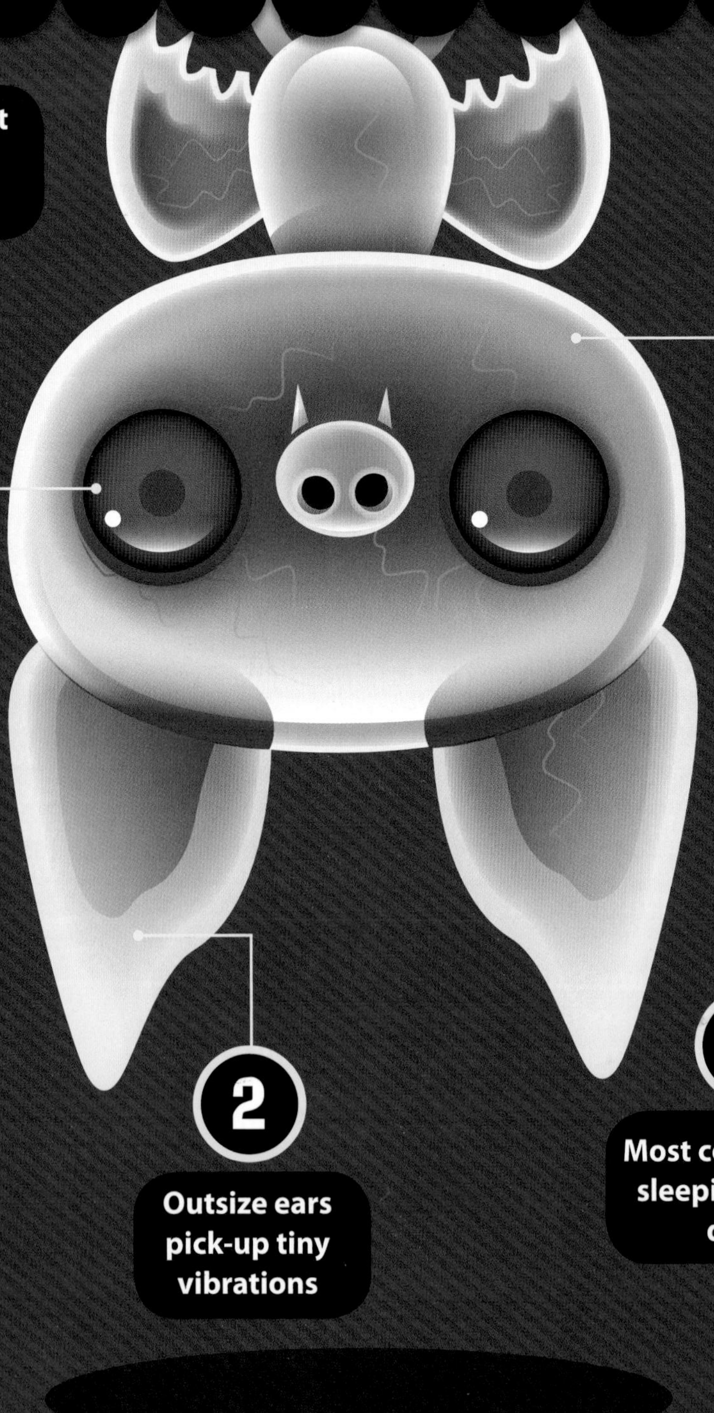

# FANTASTICALS: VAMPIRES

**Eyes don't tolerate sunlight**

**1**

**Outsize ears pick-up tiny vibrations**

**2**

**3**

**Most comfortable sleeping upside down**

**Vampire LM3RC7**

bonus
93 | 114
**Attack** 187
total **575**
**Defense** 228
**Brains** 68
34 | 46
**Tricks** 92

There's no two ways about it – Vampires are seriously spooky! These strange nocturnal critters are the stuff of legend, pasty-faced beasties that spend their days tucked out of sight in caves and ruined buildings. No matter how they mutate, the species always sleeps upside down.

This species of Fantastical has adapted itself perfectly for life in the dark. Its enlarged ears work as virtual eyes, using sound clues to suss out what lies in the shadows around it. Stepping into the sunshine is never an option. Vampires are so keen to shield their peepers that they invest any spare nuggets that they earn straight back into the sunglasses industry.

Many Vampires also have an extra power – the ability to hypnotize those around them. Although this can make the species very dangerous, they are not hard to win over. Offer a black cap to a Fantastical and you'll have made a friend for life. Just be sure not to munch on a slice of garlic bread in a Vampire's presence – the slightest whiff of the stuff offends them greatly.

**Vampire E7XBDJ**

bonus
4 | 6
**Attack** 9
total **49**
**Defense** 12
**Brains** 16
8 | 6
**Tricks** 12

# FANTASTICALS: THE UNDEAD

**Absent-minded (literally)**

**1**

**2**

**Replacement limbs**

**3**

**Body odour attracts flies**

The Undead get a bad press in FMM and yes, they totally deserve it! Grim, ghastly and utterly gruesome, these Fantasticals are never pleasant to have around. The beasties are often referred to as 'Zombies' in the common tongue – an eerie mutation with a vacant expression and an unpleasant, pungent odour.

**Phil**

| | bonus | | |
|---|---|---|---|
| **526** | 263 \| 538 | | **1k** |
| **Attack** | total | **Defense** | |
| | **3k** | | |
| **Brains** | | **Tricks** | |
| **606** | 303 \| 429 | | **858** |

This species is often accused of being empty-headed. This is absolutely fair. Most of the Undead can't help making bad decisions however, because their heads are largely empty. Many of them can even lose the bits of brain that they do have out of the holes in their skull. It's not unusual to spot a worm, fly or other small insect lurking up top instead.

**Dylan**

| | bonus | | |
|---|---|---|---|
| **104** | 52 \| 47 | | **95** |
| **Attack** | total | **Defense** | |
| | **481** | | |
| **Brains** | | **Tricks** | |
| **102** | 51 \| 90 | | **180** |

The Undead do not understand the concept of fear, so nothing scares them. They stagger anywhere that they please, but their pace is painfully slow. Unfortunately this is because a Fantastical's limbs are prone to come unattached from their body. An arm or a leg will suddenly drop onto the ground without warning. Getting the limb reattached again is a major headache.

**1**

**Undefined features**

**2**

**Body can fade into background**

**3**

**Limbs are semi-translucent**

It's easy to guess when a Spirit has drifted into the vicinity – an unexplained shiver will tingle down the spine. This ghastly species is an elusive as a Will o' the Wisp, hard to spot and almost impossible to trap in one place.

These vaporous, misty creatures move silently through the world, blending into their surroundings whenever they fancy. Their transparency can be very frustrating when trying to pin a Spirit down in conversation. Half-way through a sentence they will simply evaporate and disappear.

These Fantasticals might look like lonely critters, but appearances can be deceptive. The species won't thrive if isolated completely. Spirits like to build up a strong psychic network with other Spirits, communing regularly on a mystical level. When connecting with their friends in this way they can actually be terrible gossips. They might appear silent and vacant on the outside, but the species are living proof of the untapped power of the mind. Their telepathic prowess should never be under-estimated.

Sam

| | bonus | |
|---|---|---|
| **195** 97 | total | 79 **158** |
| Attack | **644** | Defense |
| Brains | | Tricks |
| **177** 88 | | 57 **114** |

Spirit M0HLH2

| | bonus | |
|---|---|---|
| **68** 34 | total | 28 **57** |
| Attack | **299** | Defense |
| Brains | | Tricks |
| **87** 43 | | 43 **87** |

# FANTASTICALS: DANGEROUS

**1**

**Obsessed with fairy fashion**

**Sweet appearance**

**2**

**3**

**Gossamer wings**

# FAIRIES

**Tracy**

| | bonus | |
|---|---|---|
| **112** | 56 \| 44 | **89** |
| **Attack** | total **432** | **Defense** |
| **Brains** | | **Tricks** |
| **121** | 60 \| 55 | **110** |

These minxy Monsters may look cute, but they should not be trusted under any circumstances! Dangerous Fairies are a species that always live up to their name. Many are manipulative, mean and mischievous (and that's just the nice ones).

Although they evolve into a variety of sizes and shapes, all Dangerous Fairies grow at least one pair of fine, fluttery wings. They use these to flit about all over the place causing trouble and upsetting other Monsters. When they're not making mischief, the species is almost certainly out shopping. Dangerous Fairies have an irresistible liking for gothic fashion. They can easily become distracted by a ripped purple T-shirt or black spider tights, even if there's a more pressing emergency to deal with first.

Dangerous Fairies can be tricky to defeat in battle because they aren't frightened by anything. The best method of defense therefore is distraction. If a Dangerous Fairy attacks, whip out a mirror and hold it up to their face. The creature will soon lose interest in hurting you, preferring instead to check out how pretty she is.

**Fairy VK6LQY**

Mos
O

| | bonus | |
|---|---|---|
| **88** | 44 \| 28 | **56** |
| **Attack** | total **426** | **Defense** |
| **Brains** | | **Tricks** |
| **158** | 79 \| 62 | **124** |

MONSTERS

Don't get the creeps, not all Insects are obsessed with running up trouser legs, biting humans and inflicting stings. Indeed, some are also into snapping their claws and buzzing round bedrooms, too! Insects are intriguing creatures with fierce forms and multiple, scuttling limbs. What they can't defeat with size, they'll topple with sheer volume. For Insects, power is a numbers game. Arachnids, Stingers and Super Claws all live in vast communities, joining forces to overwhelm any unfortunate that dares to step into their territory. The beastly bugs make ruthless adversaries, using their fangs, claws and pincers to inflict pain any which way they can.

**Enhanced bug vision**

**1**

**2**

**Curved pincers for grasping prey**

**3**

**Highly developed wings**

MONSTERS

Stephanie

| | bonus | | |
|---|---|---|---|
| **104** | 52 \| 95 | | **191** |
| Attack | | total | Defense |
| Brains | | 606 | Tricks |
| **186** | 93 \| 62 | | **125** |

Don't let the sleepy drone of the Stinger lull you into a false sense of security. When it comes to defending itself, this species is sharp in both wits and weapons. The mini-beast is an expert in the air, darting into action before you can say 'buzz off, bug-face!'

All Stingers have highly efficient wings. When they are airborne, even the most ingenious Monster would find them incredibly hard to catch. The species are loyal to a single Queen, flying great distances in order to carry messages for her. If their Insect monarch is at risk, they will become militant without a second's hesitation, sacrificing themselves without question for the sake of the colony. To a Stinger, the colony is everything. Those that threaten it find themselves facing thousands of enemies acting as one.

Over time, Stingers have learnt to put their quick wits to other good uses. When relaxing, the species are keen hobbyists. Many like to hone their fighting skills by fencing. Others spend their free time perfecting their aerial prowess or sharpening their sting.

Stinger ZARI5Q

| | bonus | | |
|---|---|---|---|
| **7**Ⓚ | 3k \| 5k | | **10**Ⓚ |
| Attack | | total | Defense |
| Brains | | 35 k | Tricks |
| **10**Ⓚ | 5k \| 3k | | **7**Ⓚ |

**1**

### Bulbous, pockmarked head

**2**

### Drool-producing mouth

**3**

### Limb count can vary

MONSTERS

Arachnids are much maligned in the Monster world. It's not the scuttling legs or even the creepy eyes – it's the drool. This Insect species dribbles like crazy! Other critters find this behaviour quite rude and dangerous, too. Arachnid spittle is venomous. Even the smallest spot can seep into the skin and poison the victim before they realize what has happened.

These spider-like creatures mutate into a surprisingly broad range of forms. Most, but not all, have eight limbs. It seems that many also have eight eyes, but this is rarely the case. When studied closely, the eyes turn out to be circular pockmarks dotted over the Arachnid's body. This species comes in a variety of sizes, from tiny right up to the sort of prowling Monster you'd never want to see in your bathtub, even in your worst nightmare.

Arachnid NC4WV3

| | bonus | | |
|---|---|---|---|
| | 78 | 56 | |
| 156 Attack | | 112 Defense | |
| | total 617 | | |
| Brains 213 | 106 | 68 | Tricks 136 |

Arachnids are deeply territorial – step onto their patch and they'll unleash every attack in the book. There is only one way to defeat them. The species hates hosiery. Kick out with a stocking clad leg and you might just stand a chance. Might.

Arachnid NIX312

| | bonus | | |
|---|---|---|---|
| | 53 | 79 | |
| 107 Attack | | 159 Defense | |
| | total 401 | | |
| Brains 41 | 20 | 47 | Tricks 94 |

# INSECTS: SUPER CLAWS

**Single unblinking eye**

**1**

**2**

**Claw is over-sized and sharp**

**3**

**Long limbs for maximum manoeuvrability**

Super Claw VFHQV3

| bonus | | | |
|---|---|---|---|
| 8 m | 4m | 5m | 11 m |
| **Attack** | total | **Defense** | |
| | 36 m | | |
| **Brains** | | **Tricks** | |
| 8 m | 4m | 4m | 8 m |

For this species, it really is all about the claw. Seriously! Super Claws spend their waking hours admiring, sharpening and worshipping their dangerous appendages. When they're asleep, they curl up cuddling them, ready to pounce and snap at a moment's notice.

This type of Insect displays its fighting force up front for everyone to see. All mutations have at least one super-sized claw that can be used to bite, trap and cut with shocking precision. Underestimate even the smallest Super Claw at your own risk – any derisive comments about its talon will provoke a fury that is almost impossible to quench.

For some of the species, the obsession with the claw can get totally out of control. If unchecked, the critter will waste precious hunting time polishing their snappers. They might even decide to build a shrine to celebrate all things claw-y! The species can also become narrow-minded and neurotic, constantly comparing itself to other Super Claws that parade past it. Insects that have mutated with several fine pincers love to brag to those who only have one.

Super Claw P3GFIK

| | bonus | | |
|---|---|---|---|
| 96 | 48 | 94 | 189 |
| **Attack** | total | | **Defense** |
| | 521 | | |
| **Brains** | | | **Tricks** |
| 53 | 26 | 91 | 183 |

# GENUS: ROBOTS

MONSTERS

Robots may need oiling regularly, but they have proved themselves to be just as formidable as their natural counterparts. The mechanical mutants are awesome examples of engineering, fascinating combinations of nuts, bolts and finely programmed hard drives. Robots don't have much time for emotion – most of the species are solitary characters with no need for companionship on any level. Instead the automatons focus their energies on constructing amazing homes to live in. These buildings are so creatively executed, other Monsters offer sackloads of nuggets just to stay in them. Robots can be very hard to read when fighting. Unblinking eyes and flashing lights expertly mask their strategy plans.

# ROBOTS: MECHANOIDS

**1** Hard shell protects internal wiring

**2** Eyes are expressionless

**3** Small claws for tinkering

**MechanoidLXI**

| bonus | | |
|---|---|---|
| 249 | 124 | 86 | 173 |
| Attack | total 550 | Defense |
| Brains | | Tricks |
| 69 | 34 | 29 | 59 |

Mechanoids shun company, but if kept occupied they are harmless most of the time. The little robots are happiest when they've got a spanner clamped in their claws. The species are utterly fascinated by mechanics. Their favourite thing is to find a household object and then systematically take it apart, screw by screw.

Most Mechanoid mutations evolve with at least a couple of handy claws. No matter how big the Robot, the claws are kept small enough to pick up tools. Dabbling in workshops indulges the species' love of physics. When it isn't occupied fixing machines, the Mechanoid scoots out in search of old-fashioned cars. It could tinker with the crankshafts and pistons of these classic vehicles all day long, making minor modifications and then testing them out.

The Mechanioid has such fine motor skills the rest of its body struggles to keep up. Its legs are usually small and under-developed, making it slow to escape should danger arise. Luckily most enemies soon realize that it's more useful to put the species to work fixing gadgets than bothering to try and eat it.

**Robot N429XN**

| bonus | | |
|---|---|---|
| 206 | 103 | 56 | 113 |
| Attack | total 621 | Defense |
| Brains | | Tricks |
| 190 | 95 | 56 | 112 |

# ROBOTS: SMASHER BOTS

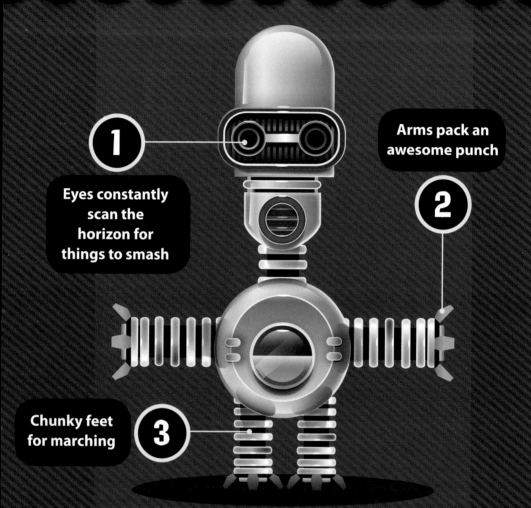

**1** Eyes constantly scan the horizon for things to smash

**2** Arms pack an awesome punch

**3** Chunky feet for marching

MONSTERS

Ask this species any question and you'll get the same answer – "Bot Smash!" This Robot exists for one purpose and one purpose alone. Every mutation is on a mission to smash anything and everything that comes across its path. Animal, vegetable or mineral, Smasher Bot will give it a smash.

Other more sophisticated species would find this lifestyle yawningly monotonous, but no Smasher Bot in the history of Smasher Bots has ever shown the slightest twitch of boredom. In fact, the crazy critters would probably give you a smash at the ludicrous suggestion of such a thing!

Smasher Bots' obsession with whacking, bopping and bashing can make them very difficult to be around. As a result they don't tend to have any friends. This is probably no bad thing – Smasher Bots are terrible conversation starters. Their perpetual punching means that they have never taken the time to read books, update their programming or learn anything new. It is commonly agreed that every rowdy Robot in the species is unbelievably dim.

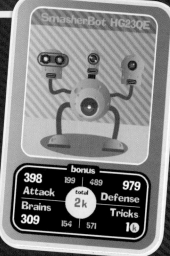

SmasherBot HG23QE

| | bonus | | |
|---|---|---|---|
| 398 | 199 | 489 | 979 |
| Attack | total | | Defense |
| Brains | 2k | | Tricks |
| 309 | 154 | 571 | 10k |

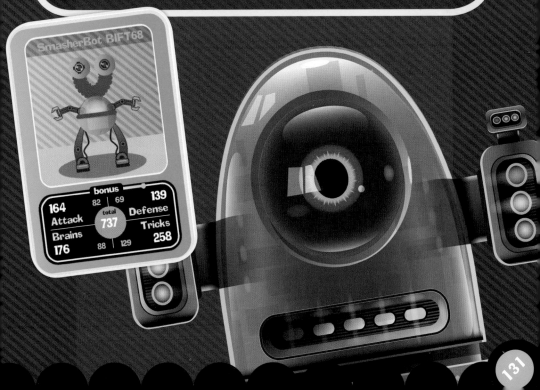

SmasherBot BIFT68

| | bonus | | |
|---|---|---|---|
| 164 | 82 | 69 | 139 |
| Attack | total | | Defense |
| Brains | 737 | | Tricks |
| 176 | 88 | 129 | 258 |

# ROBOTS: INTELLIBOTS

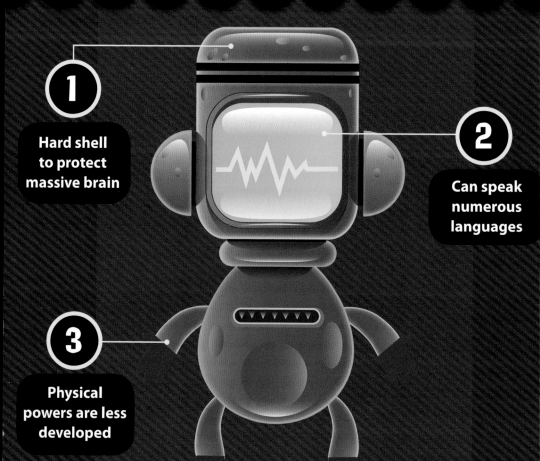

**1**
Hard shell to protect massive brain

**2**
Can speak numerous languages

**3**
Physical powers are less developed

If Smasher Bots are mentally challenged, Intellibots are right up there at the other end of the scale! These highly complex droids do not particularly enjoy being related to their strong but stupid Smasher Bot cousins. Rather than invite comparison, they choose to focus their phenomenal minds on something else instead. The Theory of Relativity, the definition of Pi and the splitting of the atom are all everyday conundrums for this Robot!

All Intellibots like to compute on a grand scale. No problem, formula or mystery is too big for them to take on. The species could theorize and plan the world's creation before you'd even finished brushing your teeth in the morning! Unfortunately, the smug droid would then spend the rest of the day congratulating itself for being so clever.

IntelliBot H2WM85

bonus
| | 50 | 42 | |
|---|---|---|---|
| **101** | | | **84** |
| Attack | | total | Defense |
| Brains | | 392 | Tricks |
| **164** | 82 | 21 | **43** |

Many Intellibot mutations are difficult to spot with the naked eye. This is because most of the significant changes take place out of sight in the Robot's cranium. It is only when the species is given a mental challenge that it gets to reveal what it can really do.

IntelliBot L7ADJO

bonus
| | 338m | 799m | 1 b |
|---|---|---|---|
| **676** m | | | |
| Attack | | total | Defense |
| Brains | | 4 b | Tricks |
| **1** b | 541m | 388m | **776** m |

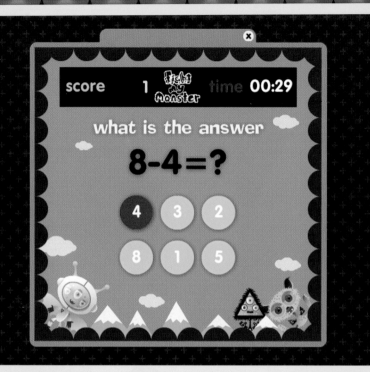

score    1    **Fight my Monster**    time **00:29**

## what is the answer

$$8-4=?$$

4   3   2

8   1   5

ARCADE

## HOW TO PLAY

Are you a number cruncher or a digit dweeb?! A few minutes on this quick-fire game will test your metal when it comes to sums. You'll need to summon up all your mental powers to answer the problems featuring addition, subtraction, multiplication and division. How many can you get through in 60 seconds?

## SUPER TIP!

Make sure your monster mouse skills are up to scratch before you start playing – quick reaction times are key when choosing from the six answer options.

## HOW TO PLAY

This cool game lets you roam the globe without ever leaving the comfort of your front room! Use your mouse to scroll around and zoom in or out to locate the countries that flick up at the top of the screen. The UK or US may not give you a headache, but what about Libya, Burma or Sri Lanka? You have 60 seconds to find up to 192 countries. Don't forget to check the side panel along the way. It will set you personal score targets to beat in order to earn yourself valuable nuggets.

time:

08:0

type this: **kit**

3
letters

no t ✓
tax ✓
but ✗ -1 sec
**kit**
mid
bin
set

restart

## HOW TO PLAY

You'll need lightning fingers to rack up the points in this game, which does exactly what it says on the tin! Type the list of words as fast and – here's the sting – as accurately as possible to win nuggets. The words start at three letters but get longer as you move down the list. Will you be typing 'antidisestablishmentarianism' when the 30 seconds are up, or will you still be picking out 'bad'?

## SUPER TIP!

Don't try re-typing a word if you get it wrong, as you'll be moved directly to the next word as soon as you hit a false key. If you try retyping, you'll only get the next word wrong too, so move on!

SCORE 14     TIME 4

## HOW TO PLAY

Rockets, space, and explosions... what's not to love? Your mission, typonaut, is to blow each rocket up before it zooms off the screen. To do this you'll need to correctly type the letter emblazoned on the rocket's core before it disappears from view. The action hots up quickly. Before you know it the sky will be filled with spacecraft to see off! One word of warning – accuracy is important as you'll lose points from your total if you type incorrect letters.

Bonus: 740     Time: 62     Score: 740

## HOW TO PLAY

There are pairs and then there are monster pairs! Give your memory a workout with this puzzle – the object of the game is to remember the positions of the identical pairs of monsters. You can only turn two virtual Fight My Monster cards over in one go and if they don't match they'll automatically turn themselves down again. The number of cards in play increases at each level, as does the amount of time you have to complete the level.

ARCADE

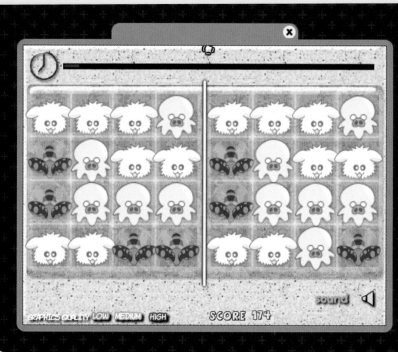

## HOW TO PLAY

Caution: this game may just send you utterly insane! On the surface it sounds simple. All you have to do is spot the difference amongst the collections of crazy creatures that appear on screen. You'll need a monstrously sharp eye to spot these subtle differences however and you have only six seconds to get each one right. Aaaaargh!

Don't clock watch. The seconds go so quickly you'll need to keep your eyes trained on the creatures themselves if you're to stand a chance of spotting the oddity each time!

141

WORD
BOSS

00:30

TIDE
SIDE
SIT

E D I T

T    S

## HOW TO PLAY
Like scrabble but got no mates to play against? Log on and give Word Boss a try. You have two minutes to make as many words of three or more letters as possible from the letter tiles you are given. Once the word is made, it appears on the board above, giving you a record of what you've spelled. Don't forget to click the tick immediately after you've formed each word – you can't waste precious seconds in this game!

## SUPER TIP!
The arrow button to the left of the game screen allows you to switch the letters around if you're having problems spotting possibilities. Make sure you pick the tiles up in the right order to spell a word – for example if you want to spell 'GULP', pick the tiles up beginning with 'G' and ending in 'P' rather than trying to put the 'G' down and slotting the 'L' in the third gap. The game automatically fills the spaces from left to right so unless you place the letters in sequence you'll lose time switching them around afterwards.

You 0:49    SparkChess 0:00

Resign Game

| 1. | c2-c4 | b7-b6 |
| 2. | e2-e3 | d7-d6 |
| 3. | Bf1-f3 | b7-b6 |
| 4. | Ng1-f3 | c7-c5 |
| 5. | e3-e4 | Nb8-c6 |

Undo Move

Save   Load

Created by weskidivision.com

## HOW TO PLAY

The three levels of Flash Chess 3 means there's a game of chess for everyone in the Fight My Monster Arcade – from novice to grand master. Choose from beginner, casual or advanced. Click on a piece to suss out your options and then click on the square you wish to move to, in order to make your move. As in the real game, once you've 'touched' a piece you have to move it!

<menu 23|25

## HOW TO PLAY

Just slide fruit around the board and you'll earn yourself a ton of points! You can only slide horizontally, but once you've created a bunch of four or more of a certain type of fruit you've got enough to make a fruit salad! Only joking – when you've got a bunch of four or more you can click on one item and make them all disappear, notching up points and eventually… nuggets. There are 20 levels to tax even the most bulging of brainiacs.

highscore: 0

## HOW TO PLAY

This memory quiz is ace for putting that grey matter to work! All you have to focus on is remembering an ever-lengthening sequence of colours. This is tougher than you might think. As the sequences get more and more monstrous, you may even have to turn down the background music to help you concentrate!

For an extra challenge, choose the Time Mode. This heaps on the pressure with a time limit and increasingly difficult symbols such as shapes, fruit and hand gestures. Do you have what it takes to earn a place on the leader board?

# Haunted House Shoot

## SCORE 0029000   TIME 12

## HOW TO PLAY

Every day is Halloween when you play this super cool shoot 'em-up game. With a range of ghosts, ghoulies and monsters for target practice, you'll never get bored! There's just one no-no. If you take a pot shot at the costumed trick or treaters, you'll be penalized by having valuable seconds subtracted from the time limit.

Don't forget to keep one eye on your ammo levels. After every five shots you'll need to click on RELOAD to get more bullets and keep on blasting.

ARCADE

All Players

146

## HOW TO PLAY

Ever wanted to get behind the wheel of a Mustang, a Corvette or an NYPD cop car? Now you can go one better. With your bird's eye view of this chaotic city junction, you get to control the approaching vehicles. Click on the cars to make them speed up, slow down or stop so that the traffic flows safely. It only takes one pile-up and it's Game Over!

## HOW TO PLAY

Ground control to Fight My Monster. Listen up! Your mission is to save astronauts stranded in space by picking them up in your rocket. The brief is so simple. Unfortunately there are black holes, meteorites and the gravitational pull of passing planets to deal with before you can bring your men home! Even the most spaced-out surfers will rely on the chilled tones of the Star Navigator music to keep it together as they progress through the tricky levels of this game.

ARCADE

## HOW TO PLAY

Ever felt like a big fish in a small pond? Or a small fish in a big one? I A Fish offers you a totally relaxing underwater gaming experience! All you've got to do is keep yourself healthy by munching on the worms and tiddlers that float by. Just cruise through the water and get nibbling! The game is over when your health fails.

## SUPER TIP!

Keep well away from any fish larger than you – even if you don't collide with them, being near them affects your karma levels. If your karma dips too low, it's bad news for your fishy health.

1891
26

B

+10

## HOW TO PLAY

Flinging a beach ball down a beach has never been so rewarding! Select your ball and use the moveable barrel to direct its trajectory. You'll need to hit the SET button at just the right moment in order to get the best angle and the maximum power. Hitting bumpers will give you an extra boost and add 10 points to your final distance. If you hit a star along the way, you'll nab 10 points and get the chance to power up your ball.

To unlock new balls with unique and varied properties you'll need to collect stars and notch up the required distance record for that ball.

## HOW TO PLAY

It's worth being a FMM member just to play this hilarious game! You are a yellow Ballie (yes, really). The aim of the game is to bump into other Ballies, but only if they're the same colour as the background. The colours change all the time – a Ballie that you should be bumping one second, is one to avoid the next. You'll know the Ballies to bump as they have a big arrow pointing at them saying BUMP ME! For extra help you can deploy one of your Ballie bombs to destroy other Ballies in your path and… oh, it's probably best if you just play it and see.

## HOW TO PLAY

Awww! Bless CaveBob, all he wants to do is jump to the top of his cave! It's an utterly perilous pastime and if he stays still too long or jumps on the wrong sort of rock platform, he dies. Use your mouse or the arrow keys to help the daring caveman leap upwards from rock to rock. When you've got to grips with play in 'Normal Mode', you'll want to try 'Challenge Mode' or the aptly named 'Impossible Mode' where perfection is the only way to win.

## SUPER TIP!

Some of the rocks move or vanish altogether and there are some not-so-nice cave-dwelling monsters to contend with along the way! Keep an eye out for the helpful dragon who'll give you a lift.

ARCADE

152

## HOW TO PLAY

If you get a kick from popping balloons, you'll be addicted to this within minutes. Click the mouse to send out circular rays of pins to pop the surrounding Ballies. Just take care to recall them with another click to avoid hitting the black, as doing so will wipe your score. In this game you can just as easily score a million points or zero within the 60-second time frame. Everything depends on avoiding that pesky black Ballie.

## HOW TO PLAY

Can you save the village from invasion by monsters? Hotshot navigational and flying skills are the key to survival! You're charged with aiming a rocket at the unwanted critters, but only a direct hit is going to be good enough to kill them. Use the arrow keys to accelerate and direct your rocket then amuse yourself for hours by working your way up the levels.

## HOW TO PLAY

Sometimes the simplest concepts are the most pleasing! This game is so easy it doesn't need instructions. Just grow your spawn by feeding on the smaller spawn that float past at the bottom of the ocean. When you spot some approaching grub, use your mouse to drag your spawn into the path of the next unsuspecting meal!

Green spawn will really help you put on some spawnal girth, but beware the shiny reds – they'll only make your spawn disintegrate and end the game.

155

46666

5

## HOW TO PLAY

Have you got turtle power? Just aim your amiable amphibian at two identical fish to 'bubble' them and remove them from play. You have two minutes to fire bubbles from the turtle, using your mouse to point him in the right direction. How many perfect pairs can you and your folks take out? It's fishy fun for all the family!

ARCADE

## HOW TO PLAY

Cloud jumping or asteroid jumping – just take your pick. Use the arrow keys to move left and right and the space bar to jump. Time your leaps perfectly and your score will climb as swiftly as you do, but jump too soon or too late and you'll be back to square one with a brand new game.

## SUPER TIP!

The concave cloud shapes and rotating asteroids mean that even when you've landed you can't rest easy, as you may roll off. Always keep looking for the next jump.

## HOW TO PLAY

Caterpillar capers are the order of the day with Weebo. Use the arrow keys to move your creepy-crawly around and feed him a fruity menu. Apples will score you 5 times the number of the level whereas watermelons will get you 30 times the level tally. The pen is small so watch out for walls, rocks and a strange cross that shortens your length!

Look out for mallets! They make you invincible and enable you to temporarily smash rocks to smithereens.

## HOW TO PLAY

Evolution itself is at the root of Cyto-Life. The aim is to grow and evolve by gathering food and avoiding or killing enemy life forms. DNA points enable you to upgrade your speed, agility and genetic make-up. Every time you go up a level you will earn one DNA point. It's monstrously mind-boggling!

OW BONUS: +120

## HOW TO PLAY

Yuri the spaceman is stranded in space – in just his boxer shorts. Can you help him find the clothes he seems to have left scattered across the universe? Use the mouse to bounce the astronaut from star to star, earning bonus points as you go. Play well and you won't be a Space Jumper noob for long!

As well as a ranking and personal best score, you can earn yourself one of Yuri's 11 achievement medals. The awards range from 'Star Starter' for lighting up at least one star all the way up to 'Maniac', given to those who score 75,000 points in a single game.

ARCADE

## HOW TO PLAY

You'll need lightning reflexes to catch the bubbles in this game. The orbs zip across the screen at super speed! In order to gain points you have to click and hold not one, but two of the little blighters. It's all bubbletastic fun devised by brainiacs to send you boggle-eyed – just don't get too greedy!

## HOW TO PLAY

Reckon you've got what it takes to cut it as an ally drone stuck deep in hostile territory? Now's your chance to prove it! You've been charged with causing chaos for the enemy on a massive scale. Create maximum mayhem by hovering over enemy tank command and turning the vehicles against each other. Simply click on a tank to take control and move your mouse to train the gun turret on the others. There's no time limit – just keep on shooting until they've destroyed each other! Look out for the ammo icons – they give you super firepower.

### SUPER TIP!

When two tanks collide they overheat. WARNING: This can cause you to lose a life if you don't blow them up immediately!

ARCADE

162

TRY TO LIMIT THE AMOUNT OF LAUNCHED BOMBS =OR= FUN PLAY!!!

BOMB DROP   SCORE   BONUS 966

## HOW TO PLAY

Tsk! Owning a flying island is no fun at all when it gets over-run with pesky robots! Your mission in this game is to clear a whole skyful of floating atolls by destroying every droid that you see. Take to the air in your chopper, line up your sights then click the mouse to drop bombs over the Boozoids below. Every single robot has to be wiped out for each level to be completed.

## HOW TO PLAY

Breaker, breaker – got your ears on? Gotta big load for the big road! Wannabe truckers are going to lurrrvvve this driving game. The cool canyon backdrop just adds to the atmosphere! Can you safely deliver your load to the depot? You'll need to go steady over rickety bridges and accelerate up hillsides to get there without losing your cargo. You could have anything onboard – from giant boulders to clattering crates or even a towering tree trunk. You'll need to control your speed to unlock cool new trucks and levels.

ARCADE

## HOW TO PLAY

There's actually very little that's retro about this space game! From the techno sound track to the cool graphics, it gives a classic a whole new high-octane spin. Use your mouse to move your ship around the playfield, taking out the invaders coming at you in their droves. You can obtain weapon upgrades and bombs by collecting floating POWER ORBS. You have 3 lives and 90 levels to blast through, so you could be here for some time!

You can only gain the achievements if you don't use any of the three possible 'continues' available in each game.

# Blockies Breakout

## HOW TO PLAY

Are you one of those people who can rub your tummy and pat your head at the same time without even thinking about it? If so you'll find Blockies Breakout a breeze! Great hand/eye co-ordination is the name of this game. You've just got to move your Blockie left or right to deflect the cute little moving square and take out the rows of Blockies moving down on your head. Succeed and you'll earn extra nuggets, but beware – Blockies is highly addictive!

ARCADE

## HOW TO PLAY

It's time to choose from a Freefighter, a Tricraft Lithium or a Cylium Hunter and cruise around the galaxy killing aliens. Sounds daunting? Luckily each craft comes with a helpful co-pilot. Listen to their advice and, if you destroy enough bad guys, you get the princess! Awesome!

### SUPER TIP!

You can move position as well as swivel using specified keys on the keyboard – just follow your co-pilot's instructions. He'll also take you through your ship's special features.

## HOW TO PLAY

Test your zen in this mystical challenge from the Orient. During your quest to collect golden gaming nuggets, there are invaluable words of wisdom from the great Chinese thinker Confucius to pick up as as you play. Manoeuvre your snake carefully in order to power up the portal to the next level – strange entities will do their best to stop you getting there.

Every time your snake touches a green energy ball, a section gets added its tail. Each section represents a life, but as your tail gets longer it becomes harder to move around!

ARCADE

168

## HOW TO PLAY

Watch out for the slippy poo on the track at the Skidmark Cup! The yucky stuff will send you into a spin on contact. This 3D karting game offers full-on fun for FMM speed junkies, challenging your driving skills to the max! As you skid round the track, collect capsules and boost your chances with extra power-ups. Some will give you a boosty bean fuelled burst of speed, others bowl a skulling ball to strike out your rivals. Grab as many gold Skid MKs coins as you can, then use them to buy stuff in the virtual shop.

## HOW TO PLAY

Those cute round Ballies are back, but this time they're shooting at you! Move left or right to hit as many of the spherical so-and-sos as you can. The attacking Ballies will obligingly drop fruit for you to gulp, so make sure you gobble as many point-boosting grapes, berries and cherries as you can. Stay alert however – occasionally those devilish Ballies will decide to drop a bomb instead. Double gulp!

## SUPER TIP!

If you're wondering which of the keys is the 'fire' button, the answer is none of them. Your Ballie fires automatically – you just have to make sure it's floating in the right place to hit something!

ARCADE

## HOW TO PLAY

If you liked Retro Shoot, you're going to go monster mad for Retro Shoot 360! The fate of the Earth depends on one lone encounter between a single astro pilot and an evil alien armada of Retronauts. Guess what FMM gamers? The pilot they've drafted in is YOU! Prepare yourself for the fight of your life as alien craft attack from every angle. The backstory is brilliant and guess what, you're not even allowed to play until you can cut it in the trainer simulator! Cool!

# Gold Of Pirate Bay

All Players

**ARCADE**

## HOW TO PLAY

Are you ready to jump in your submarine pod and dive down into the big blue? You're Jimmy the diver and it's your job to search the ocean depths, collecting gold coins for your Captain. Every time you find a coin, you'll need to tow it back to a waiting magnet so it can be hauled up into the Cap's airship. There are undersea caves and caverns to explore – as long as your oxygen supply holds out! Watch out for deadly sea creatures and take care not to sink into the abyss.

### SUPER TIP!

Float past the air tanks and heart icons to buy more time below the waves.

172

## HOW TO PLAY

Missile Rush has three perilous modes – Arcade, Asteroid and Smartbomb. Whichever you choose, you're about to unleash the fight of your life. It's time to defend civilization as you know it against a barrage of incoming missiles. The enemy has gone for a stealth attack, bombarding your defenses under the cover of nightfall. It's up to you to guard the city skyline, shooting down as many attackers as you can. Good luck!

# Antidote Pandemia

## HOW TO PLAY

Ew! A nasty virus is threatening to get out of control, unless you can zap the germs before they multiply. You'll need quick reactions and eyes in the back of your head to ward off this gruesome micro-enemy. The good news? Each germ makes a truly satisfying squish when it bites the dust at the end of one of your lasers. You can also upgrade your ammo and weapons at each new level. Will your quick thinking and lightning reflexes prevent a pandemic?

The larger and uglier the germ, the more ammo it takes to squelch it into oblivion!

**ARCADE**

That's all folks. Go fight!

# GROD

commands you to visit

## monsterfun.com!
## All hail GROD!